PROSE, POETRY & PROPHECY

PROSE
POETRY & PROPHECY

A THRILLING AND PASSIONATE NARRATIVE OF CHRIST AND HIS CHURCH

```
                C
        C               C
                R
    E           O       O
                S
E               S           W
D               S           N
```

"FOR ONE GREATER THAN SOLOMON IS HERE"

Copyright © 2010 by Barbara K. Carey.

ISBN:	Softcover	978-1-4415-9708-3
	Ebook	978-1-4415-7852-5

All rights reserved. No part of this book may be reproduced or transmitted in any form or by any means, electronic or mechanical, including photocopying, recording, or by any information storage and retrieval system, without permission in writing from the copyright owner.

This book was printed in the United States of America.

To order additional copies of this book, contact:
Xlibris Corporation
1-888-795-4274
www.Xlibris.com
Orders@Xlibris.com

I
AM THE

ROSE OF SHARON, THE LILY OF THE VALLEY

AND

MY BANNER OVER YOU IS LOVE

DEDICATION

Running with my 200, I dedicate this Book,

to my Four children: Sharon, Ted, John and Don,

holding faith that they would pass it on to their children,

in the generations to come.

With all my love

Mother

CONTENTS

Introduction

Chapter I   God Walked Among His Garden Trees

Chapter II   The Apple Tree

Chapter III   The Fig Tree

Chapter IV   The Palm Ree

Chapter V   The Pomegranate Tree

Chapter VI   The Clusters Of Grapes

Chapter VII   The Barley Grain

Chapter VIII   Mandrakes

Chapter IX   Nuts And Chief Spices

Chapter X   Our Little Sister Without Breast

Chapter XI   Running The Race To Receive The Crown

Chapter XII   The 800 Meters

Chapter XIII   Lowering The Bar, Raising The Standard

Chapter XIV   The Faith Run

Chapter XV   The Three Hundred Meters

Chapter XVI   The Home Stretch

INTRODUCTION

Conceived and birthed in the vestibule of spiritual disgrace, allegiance and submission, the great Monarch rose from a descent of betrayal, adultery and murder to ascend the Throne of Israel as the wisest man that ever lived. Chosen by Divine Providence, a Merciful God is revealed through the chronicles of compassion, long-suffering and Love. For Love is the very Foundation of the narrative of Solomon's Song as he serenaded Jesus Christ, the World's greatest Lover and His Beloved, His Woman, His Church, His Body through the annals of Prophecy.

To have and to hold, One must look beyond the atavism of the flesh to the ONE, the owner of the Garden, the One who alone qualifies as "The ROSE OF SHARON, AND LILLY OF THE Valley. Yes! Nazareth's dirty, mucky valley, out of which that ONE so pure and holy shone; so white and so bright, as the Fairest of ALL the heavenly Host. For His Love is as Strong as Death and His Jealousy as CRUEL as the Grave. Hence the call, inviting all flesh to the Banquet of all the ages in the celestial realm of the Divine Triad, the Husbandman of the Garden Temple.

Meet the Apple and Fig Trees and understand the call to return to the "stature of the Palm Tree", with "the tender Grapes that appeared", and the" Pomegranate that budded". Understand how the Appointed Barley of "Three measures" must be blended with the "Principal Wheat", of one measure, all for a penny. And understand how Y O U! "a keeper of the Fruit of the Garden must have your 200". For if YOU are not a grain of Wheat, sad will be YOUR lot as a sprig of Tare, when the "Three Measures of Barley" returns; and God walks through His Garden Temple again, as Eden is restored and man can once more gaze upon the Face of the Almighty God and live to enjoy the pleasures of HIS Perfection.

For as it was in the Beginning, so will it be in the END; when "the Lord God and the Lamb will again become the Temple" at that Day, just as the Two Trees stood in the Midst of the Garden in the Beginning.

CHAPTER ONE

GOD WALKED AMONG HIS GARDEN TREES

There are Two Immutable Things, that makes it impossible for God to Lie and they "are the Immutability of His Counsels" (Heb 6:17-18), the Two Tables of Commandments; by HIS "Two Faithful Witnesses" (Rev 11:3-12), the Two Olive Trees. They depict Jesus as the Two Cherubs, the WORD of God, The Old and New Testaments. For the Cherubs were made out of the Olive Tree Wood (1 Kg 6:23), depicting Jesus as "the Two Faithful Witnesses" (Rev 11:3-12). Henceforth, Jesus declared:

> "search the scriptures, ... for they
>
> testify of Me: and "if you want to know about Me,
>
> Learn of ME, through the Prophets and the Psalms"
> (Lk 24:27,44 Jn 5:39).

For it is not flesh that attains, but God Who ordains and endows. Hence the greatness of the men and women, whom God Almighty has chosen to live out His Plan and Purpose; including Jesus His Beloved Son, was accomplished by Divine Providence. For it is written:

> "All this was done that was spoken by the prophets
>
> Concerning ME" (Mt 1:22, 2:15,23)

Therefore, in order to prosper in the things of God we must "believe the prophets" (2 Ch 20:20), for God does nothing unless HE reveals it to His Servants, and prophets" (Am 3:7). And so by God's Two Immutable Tables defining His Counsels, HE spoke in the Beginning and HE is still bringing IT to pass today and always. For HE is God, the WORD without Beginning and Ending of Days" (Heb 7:3); and no barrier of Time can prevent His Purpose from being fulfilled. Mankind come, and are made great by the Great I AM, then they go off the scene. For the "grass withers and the flower fades" (1 Pe 1:24), but GOD and His WORD {Jesus Christ} lives on forever.

So, although David's heart was perfect toward God, yet he was not chosen for the building of God's House in the Earth. No! not because of his many flaws of earthen foolishness which God pardoned, because He honored and reverenced his God, submitting himself unto HIM after his foolish acts of betrayal. But rather because David was a man of war with bloody hands; and as such, he could not build the Temple of the LORD although His killing was in favor of God. For the Temple of the Lord, by its very nature has been etched in BLOOD, prophetically from the Foundation of the WORLD; and that BLOOD was the righteous and undefiled substance of :

"The LAMB slain from the Foundation

Of the WORLD" (Rev 13:8)

Henceforth, Solomon a seed of that bloody man David, with clean hands and a pure heart, was chosen to build God's earthly temple house; until the True Temple Builder, the Sure Foundation (Is28:16), the Chief Corner Stone came and destroyed that Earthly Temple, to set HIMSELF UP, as the TEMPLE of His Own Body, by His Own BLOOD. For:

"In three days, I will destroy THIS Temple

and raise up a brand new Temple in My

Own Body" (Jn 2:19-21)

Repairing the Breach, restoring the Path, fulfilling the Law, and today HE is **still** perfecting the Promise, [a PROMISE that many Faith Warriors have waited for from the days of Abel to this present time, **but** have **not** yet received (Heb 11:4-39). For God is still "providing THAT better thing for us" (V 40); before Jesus comes again to bring in Peace among the Trees of HIS Garden Temple, thus restoring Eden. No! Solomon could not rule Israel peaceably, without special endowment, for the War was not without, but within. Two Women, a woman of truth and a woman of lies and deceit claiming the same Child. But because of the cleanness of his heart, Solomon's request, pleased God and God honored him, giving him all wisdom and spiritual understanding. And today we too are called to such an order:

"that we might be filled with the knowledge of H**is**

Will in all wisdom and spiritual understanding" (Col 1:9-10)

Moreover, this knowledge was not the worldly wisdom of scientific, technological or academic pursuits of excellence; and or professional commendation to be conferred, for Solomon was also given a 'bonus' package of all Wealth, Power and Prosperity in addition to His request. Therefore he did not need to wise up to this world's struggle for success and recognition. And because of God's endowment, Solomon was able to settle the matter of the two women wisely, honoring the true mother, the virtuous woman. But today these Two women are still prophetically and spiritually at war, claiming the same Man child, for God **still** regards His Church as "a WOMAN comely and delicate" (Jer 6:2).

Henceforth, the two women depicted by Solomon's wisdom stand today prophetically and spiritually. See them as the Pure Woman of Truth with the Moon under her feet, clothed in the Sun, bearing a Man Child " (Rev 12:1-5). She is a woman of light, enthralled with the Two Great Lights of God (Gen 1:14-17); distinguishing Her from Creation, as God's Woman{His Remnant Church today}; thus setting Her apart from the Seven women of darkness: "seven UNRULY women who want to hold on to one man [the Man Child], just to cover themselves" (Is 4:1). Women of lies and deceit, the daughters of "the Mother of harlots, clothed in silk, satin and costly array"(Rev 17:1-5); and these make up the Seven women of the Seven dispensations of the Earth that oppose God. For as there were "Seven Churches of God, by the Seven Candlesticks" (Rev 1:11-20), there were also Seven Churches by the Beast Power, ruled by Man(Rev 17:1-9).

Thus the Wisdom of God is distinguished between the two kinds of knowledge, taken from the tree of good and evil which was instituted in the Beginning and placed in the Midst of the Garden of the Lord (Gen 2:15-17). And today we {of Laodicea, the LAST Prophetic Church} are also called to such an Understanding, because it affects us physically, prophetically and spiritually. So:

"get wisdom and get knowledge but in all thy
getting, get understanding" (Pro 4:4-8).
And "let him who read understand" (Mt 24:14-15).
Understand that the first two Nations are no more:
that "these two nations and these two countries shall
be Mine, whereas the Lord WAS there" (Ezek 35:10).
Yet they affect us of the THIRD **Part** today by
{430 x 3 = 1290} to bring us to our heritage. (Dan 12:11).

And {430} constitute the Pilgrimages of God's Four Chief

Princes: Abraham {130} - Isaac {130} - Jacob {130} - Jesus {40}

{130 x 3 = 390}   <   Ezek 4:4-6   >   {390 + 40 = 430}

Which was confirmed by Jesus (Gal 3:14-17).

Oh the ecstasy of the Man lying between His two breasts "her two breasts are like roes" (SS 4:5) and there HE lie all night, sleeping comfortably in the Wake of the Cross. For LOVE is as strong as Death and JEALOUSLY as cruel as the grave" (SS 8: 6). But *there between* the TWO, He proved His Love for His Beloved, Y O U. That HE may set His Seal upon Y O U, to claim YOU as His very own. Nevertheless it all began with the two daughters of one woman: Aholah and Aholibah, because "THEY WERE MINE" (Ezek 23:1-4).

Hence the two horns of the prophetic ram of the Sanctuary that was broken, with the last horn rising higher" (Dan 8:7); depicting Jesus Christ and His two women as Joint Heirs" (Eph 3:6, Ro 8:17). Yea, twins by their two breasts, for Jerusalem and Samaria were joined together by the CROSS. But, Jesus "cut-off these TWO" (Zech 13:8-9) when HE was "cut-off in the midst" (Dan 9:27); dying between these two nations, two countries, two dispensations thus, wiping them out through HIS Death and simultaneously raising up the THIRD

Part: "the Remnant of the Gentiles" a people that are left in the Land today. Understand, that while the Third Part is not joined with the first two parts as joint heirs physically, it is connected, prophetically and spiritually, for HE has made them One:

"no more Jews and no more Gentiles,

For I have made you, ONE" (Gal 3:28-29)

And this constitutes HIS Woman, His Beloved, whom Solomon serenaded with symbols of prophetic jargon. For the THINGS of God are foolishness to man, even as "the Wisdom of man is foolishness to God" (1 Co 3:19). But "ONE greater than Solomon is now here" (Mt 12:42), hear HIM.

Therefore, let us seek to understand the Wisdom of God's Seven Trees that are still in His Garden. A Garden that HE locked and barred up, well-guarded by Cherubim and Flaming Swords; after driving the Man Adam OUT into the Field {the Field is the World Mt 13:38} to live and work among thorns. No! God's Trees were not the well loved avocado, orange, or mango trees of this earthen planet but Trees that has significant meaning to our Salvation through Jesus Christ. Hence, it was this spiritual "wisdom and understanding" (Col 1:8-10); that Solomon sung about as he serenaded Jesus Christ and His Beloved, His Church, His Body.

Let us now meet the ONE, who raised US up under the Apple Tree. For: HIS Love is Strong and HIS Jealousy is *still cruel* as the *grave*. For He has proven Himself, "laying down His Life for His Church, His Beloved,

Y O U!

CHAPTER TWO

THE APPLE TREE

His work was finished after the First Six Days of Creation. Then God made a day for Himself and rested on HIS Day, which "HE blessed, sanctified and set apart" (Gen 2:1-3) from the Six days that He made for man. No! God was not tired that HE needed to REST, because HE speaks and it is done, He commands and it comes to pass and stands fast. But, HE rested Spiritually [enjoining]in communion with His Son Adam {and today all flesh}. Henceforth man who was created on the **SIXTH** day, stands by his Number {6} from Creation. Then God planted a Garden, Eastward in Eden and called it the Garden of Eden and there HIS Voice was heard walking through HIS Garden in the Cool of the Day to commune with His children (Gen 2:8, 3:8). It must be understood, however that the **EAST** was, is and always will be God's Domain, where His Presence dwells (Ezek 43: 1-3). Thus it was that, "that the Righteous Man was raised up from the East (Is 41:2-4), for the First Time, "we have seen His Star in the East" (Mt 2:2). And when HE comes again the Second Time, He will also descend Like lightening from the East" (Mt 24:27).

Therefore, God's Garden Temple {His Church} was in the Eas**t,** where HE placed the Man, Adam. And it was in this Garden, God's Domain, His Holy Temple where His Voice walked daily among His Trees. Moreover, today in Prophecy and in the Sanctuary, the EAST is still where the Good "Tidings [of the Gospel go forth from the Church of God that] "troubles the Beast" [Satan] (Dan 11:44). And so after Eve transgressed and Adam sinned, as a result of the Serpent's iniquity, the WORD went forth:

"Because you have made your iniquity to be remembered, your

Transgressions were discovered and your Sin appeared, . . . so you shall be taken with the hand and that profane wicked

prince . . . . shall have an END" (Ezek 21:24-25).

Yes Satan and Sin with all sinners will have an end, because JESUS came, and finished the Work, His Six Point Mission Agenda:

(1) He finished the TRANSGRESSION: Crying as HE exhaled His last earthly breath: "IT IS FINISHED" (Jn 19:30)

(2) He made an END of SIN: It "has no more Dominion over us . . ." (Ro 6:14)

(3) He made RECONCILIATION for iniquity: "By the Cross" (Eph 2:16)

Then He was crucified and arose:

(4) To bring in everlasting righteousness.

(5) To seal the Vision.

(6) To anoint the Most Holy" (Dan 9: 2 4).

Thus putting an End to the THREE culprits who brought about man's downfall. And by these THREE acts of betrayal, we can understand David's Plea (Ps 51:1-2):

"Blot out my transgression   Wash me from my sin,

Purge me from my Iniquity"

And today, all flesh suffer the same fate as a result of the Woman's Transgression, the Man's Sin, and the Serpent's Iniquity in Eden.

And so God Almighty drove the Man Adam out of His Garden Temple [the Church]; and guarded His Trees by closing and barring up the GATE with Cherubs and Flaming Swords; thus removing IT out of the reach of sinful man. For it must be understood, that the "GATE" represents the House of God: "this is none other than the House of God and the GATE of Heaven" (Gen 28:17). Hence the Flaming Sword was put in Place to turn into every WAY, of Succeeding Generations **[and there are only FOUR major Generations, with many sub-generations]**; to reveal the Temple Presence of the Lord, by His Two Cherubs. For the Trees of God's Garden Temple were not the ordinary trees of the World but rather symbolic Trees of Righteousness. Hence the Two Cherubs were put in place to guard them:

CHERUBIMS	FLAMING SWORDS
Projected Jesus	Projected Ministers of God
The WORD by the symbol	who preach the Word, and
of the Olive Tree Wood	represents Jesus as flames of fire
(1 Kg 6:23, Rev 11:3-12)	(Ps 104:4)

Moreover, the Trees in God's Garden Temple stood in Order of *sequence* and *significance* by the Divine Mandate. The First Tree of God's Garden was HIS Apple Tree, a symbol of God's Love and His Law; the Foundation of His Government in Heaven and Earth.

"Keep my commandments and live,
My Law as the APPLE of your
Eye, bind them upon thy finger {ten fingers,
depicting the ten
Precepts} and write them upon the table of your
Heart. Say unto wisdom thou art my sister and call
Understanding thy kinswoman, that they may keep
Thee from the Strange Woman" (Pro 7:1-5).

So sing your Song Solomon, "for as the Apple Tree is among

the woods so is My Beloved among the sons:

I sat down under HIS

Shadow with great delight and his fruit was sweet to my

taste. He brought me to the banquet table, and His banner over me is L O V E.
Stay with Me flagons,
comfort Me with apples, I am sick for L O V E"(SS 2:1-5).

And so if we hold and keep God's commandments as the apple of our eye, then we can confidently ask of God to "keep ME {us} as the apple of HIS eye; and "hide me under the shadow of thy wings" (Ps 17:8, Dt 32:10). Love is a two way affair with each of the parties giving their all to honor the wishes of the two within the UNION by word and example. So! "if you say you know ME and keep not MY Commandments, you are a liar and there is no truth in you" (1 Jn 2:3). If you love Me, keep My Commandments" (Jn 14:15, 21-25).

Love speaks action, "If you Love Me, prove it.
"Love is powerful and

Strong as Death; and Jealously is as cruel as the Grave,

many waters cannot quench it and

the floods cannot drown it" (SS 8:6-7).

I proved My LOVE for You, will you do any less for Me?

Don't you know that I am jealous over Y O U! "I am a

Jealous God over my Creation. My very "Name is Jealousy" (Ex 20:5, 14)

for I raised you UP under the Apple Tree" (SS 8:5), in My

Garden, that you may learn to obey ME.

And even after you have sinned and destroyed my Fig Tree, I gave you My Pomegranate, My grapes and My barley; dying for You! Just to prove how much I love you, My Beloved. So I can place My Banner over You to Seal You. Let Me "set My SEAL upon YOU, even as you set Me as a Seal upon your heart"(SS 8:6): "for the Foundation of

God has THIS SEAL, God knows HIS own"(2 Ti 2:19). And, didn't God place His SEAL literally, in the midst of His Law, bearing His Name, as LORD GOD, His Title as CREATOR GOD and His Territory over which HE rules as HEAVEN and EARTH? For everything that belongs to God carries His Seal of Approval and Ownership; just as the Seals of every earthly potentate bears their Name, Title and the Scope of their Authority.

So when God puts His Seal upon YOU! You become His by:

CREATION   SALVATION   REDEMPTION.

I AM the ONE who planted the Apple Tree, setting up MY LAW as "Creator and Lawgiver" (Jam 4:12). Don't you know that I AM Jesus, My Father's **Right Hand**, the ONE WHO gave you "the Law on Mount Sinai" (Dt 33:1-4) by the Hand of Moses? Yes the SAME One who says: "I will uphold YOU with the **Right Hand** of My Righteousness (Is 41:10).

And now behold the Man!

for today, ONE Greater than Solomon is HERE" (Mt 12:42)

"JUDGE, LAWGIVER, SAVIOR and KING" (Is 33:22).

Yes! I AM *J E S U S*

***Rose of Sharon, Lilly* of the Valley**

Come into My Garden, My Beloved and feed ME with apples, "for My Beloved is Mine and I am His "(SS 2:16). I AM SICK FOR YOUR L O V E!

CHAPTER THREE

THE FIG TREE

O lament for her, "how did she become tributary"

weeping sore in the night for comfort.

no apples, no comfort, for only Apples can bring ME comfort,

and if I have no comfort My Beloved, how can you?

For "hath this been in your days or even in the days of your

Fathers, you would have told your children

and let them tell their children and

on and on, to the children that hath not

yet been born, from generation to generation"
(Jl 1:4, Ps 78:5-8)

Yes Adam! where art thou, and why are you afraid? Why have you gone into hiding? Didn't "I raised you up under the Apple Tree" (SS 8:5)? And gave you My Law. Have you exploited Me, and broken My Commandments, and defiled My Temple? Have you attacked My fig tree, seeking peace: "where there is no peace" (Jer 6:14); and are you looking for cover under My fig leaves? You said you were naked; but I clothed you with My Glory. Have you lost your glorious clothing? Do you not know that you cannot hide your sins, My Son:

"acquaint yourself with God and be at Peace" (Job 22:21),
for blessed is he whose sins are covered" (Ps 32:1).

But Lord, it's the woman that did it, the same one that YOU gave to me. She gave me the fruit and I did eat"

"Woman!

What is this that you have done"? (Gen 3:9-13).

Yes! Woman, Woman, Woman, that is what Jesus called them even when He was speaking to His Beloved Mother, it was still woman. "Woman what is it to Me, my hour has not yet come, Woman where are your accusers, woman great is thy faith". For that was all that Adam's Woman had become when She transgressed; and lost it all in that brief moment of curiosity and deception. Yes she sinned first, but she loved greatest. "Woman why are you weeping, whom are you seeking"? And right there, at the sound of His Voice, the woman was ready to surrender to her Lord and Master. For she who hath sinned the most, sensed the greatest need for love and acceptance. "Mary! Touch Me not, but *go* and *tell* . . ." Yes, the woman had been liberated, released from "under the rule" of (Gen 3:15-16) and restored as a Daughter in Equal standing with her counterpart. For she has been called by her own Name, and given her mission, ordained to "go and tell", hence the Church's Mission to tell the Good News.

And so, holy war broke out in the Garden of the Lord, for though it was the woman who transgressed, it was the Man Adam [the Priest] who sinned and broke his Father's Commandments. Yea, "he that know to do good, and do it not, to Him it is sin" (Jam 4:17). For "it was the Commandments of God that made the Garden as Peaceful as a River"(Is 48:18). So that, when Adam disobeyed just once and broke God's Law, he offended Jesus Man # 7, the LAWGIVER and CREATOR HIMSELF ; ten {10} times {7x10=70}. Therefore, touching one tree, sent a rippling effect throughout the whole Garden, destroying all the trees. For to break one command, is to offend and be found guilty of them all (Jam 2:10).

And so, after our Father Adam sinned, he had to be cut-off at {930} yrs, SEVENTY {70} years short of a {1000}, thus instituting the Sanctuary of Seventy {7 x 10 = 70}, which represents Jesus, as the ONLY Savior, and offering for Sin in the Sanctuary. For the WAY back to God Almighty, is in the Sanctuary (Ps 77:13). Hence Jesus became our SANCTUARY bearing the WEIGHT of all the SINS of the World in the BOWL at the top of the Candlestick. And that Silver Bowl which weighed {70} shekels (Num 7:11-13), represents all the confessed sins of every repentant sinner from the Beginning to the End. Hence the Seventy of the Sanctuary, by days, weeks, months, years or things symbolically represents Jesus Christ, to all the World as Creator, Lawgiver and Savior (Is 33:22, Jam 4:12).

Therefore, Adam had to be cut-off at {930 yrs}. And to be cut off was to die and lose out on the Ambience of the Glorious Perfection, the Presence of all Three Persons of the Godhead. And this United Presence constitutes the THOUSAND YEARS {1000 - 930 = 70}, the ONE THNG that all flesh must **not** be ignorant of:

1 — **One Godhead {All Three Persons}**

0 — **God the Father—Equal Person**

0 — **God the Son [WORD]—Equal Person**

0 — **God the Holy Ghost—Equal Person**

Thus it is written "BE NOT IGNORANT OF this one thing . . ." (2 Pe 3:8). And so flesh cannot earn or achieve the [70]; whether it was by Weeks of the Earthly Sanctuary, or by Years of the Heavenly Sanctuary. For the Seventy is Part and Parcel of the WHOLE: {930 + 70= 1000}, representing the Ambience [Presence]of the Godhead.

Hence our Seventy Years Prophetic Time Period today is connected to the thousand [1000] years of (Ps 90:4-12). Adam broke IT, and Jesus came and fixed IT, giving us "a DAY for a year" (Ezek 4:3-6), for God holds the {1000} years, as a day, the Prophetic Day of Salvation.

Oh! So you thought that there was a literal River of Water in Eden, that parted to produce Four? No, more than there is a literal River Presence today in this Generation, "the Great River Euphrates", the last and Greatest of the Four Rivers, featured in the Revelation of Jesus Christ, our River Head of this End Time Generation (Rev 9:14).

For, when Sin made its entrance, the Most High God made His exit and with Him went His River Presence. For it is GOD'S Tabernacle Presence that stands as a River:

"There is a River, the streams whereof shall make glad

the City of God, the Holy Place of the Tabernacle of the Most High,

for GOD is in the midst of HER, She shall not be move:" (Ps 46:4-5).

Well! isn't God still "visiting the earth today with HIS River Presence, watering it and preparing our corn" (Ps 65:9-13). Metaphorically, as HE provides our Daily Bread? (Ps 65:9-13). Thus it must be understood that the River of Eden, out of which the Four Rivers came, was prophetic with significance pointing to God's Government in the Earth, by His tabernacle Presence, His ability to provide for Adam, as HE provides for us today: Jehovah JIREH, our Provider, Jehovah RAPHA, our healer, Jehovah SHAMMAH, our strength, Jehovah NISSI, our Protector, Jehovah SHALOM our Peace, the Almighty God, our Father.

And isn't He still providing to "the Third and Fourth generations, that HE is visiting" (Num 14:18, Ex 20:5)? For the third and fourth generations stand together; as the First and Second generation stood in time; divided by the flood of water, to climax with a flood of fire. Hence His Four Riverheads [His Four Chief Princes], as leaders over His people in the Earth, each in his own dispensation; with Jesus being the LAST of them all, Riverhead today of the Great Euphrates, our Fourth Generation. For as it was in the beginning, God's Presence will always flow forth from His

Throne, from River to River:

ONE RIVER in the Garden   < G O D >   ONE RIVER in the City
Two trees standing in the Midst   Two trees standing in the Midst
   Gen 2:8-10 *   THE EARTH   HEAVEN Rev 22:1-2

So! "is God angry with the rivers [a body of water], Was His Wrath against the Sea, a body of water" (Hab 3:8). Absolutely not, God is not angry at a body of natural water. He is displeased and angry at Sin and sinners who hold on to Sins. For Water in prophecy whether in a River bed or the ocean of the Sea, represents people, multitudes and nations" (Rev 17:15).

Hence God's Four Prophetic Rivers Vs His Four Part Prophetic Beast, representing the CHURCH by the Riverheads and the WORLD by the Four Part Beast (Dan 2:23-44), yea Church and State by His chosen leaders:

CHURCH				STATE [THE World]		
RIVER	**RIVERHEAD**	**BOUNDRY**	**-**	**EMPIRE**	**BEAST**	**WORLDLEADER**
Pison	Abraham	Egypt	-	Babylon	Gold	Nebuchadnezzar
Gihon	Isaac	"SAME"	-	Medes/Persia	Silver	Cyrus/Darius
Hiddekel	Jacob	Assyria/Ethiopia	-	Greece	Brass	Alexander, the Gr.
Great Euphrates	Jesus	Boundless river - All Nations		Rome	Legs of	Iron & Clay all the World

Albeit, it was the mist that watered the earth until the flood, not the river, and today we have the rainfalls that waters the earth. And so you have attacked My Fig Leaves, and destroyed My Fig Tree, My symbol of Peace, Jehovah SHALOM. Is there any wonder why Jesus was ready to curse the barren fig tree? For man's sinful covering cannot hide them from shame and disgrace, hence the barrenness that filtered down to the house of Israel, by the THREE barren Women of the Covenant, "kindling Jacob's anger" (Gen 30:1-2), and destroying their Peace.

Yes! Woman "what is THIS that you have done" (Gen 3:13), now a spotless Lamb must die to provide a covering for sin. For "without the shedding of blood there is no remission of sin" (Heb 9:22). And where Sin, abides, the Peace of God cannot be found. No, not Fig leaves Adam, BLOOD. Blood is the only THING that appeases My anger: and "My anger smokes like a furnace" (Ps 74:1). Hence the SMOKING FURNACE {God Almighty} Who cannot look upon sinful man without the "BURNING LAMP" {Jesus the WORD} Gen 15:16-18. For "thy WORD is a Lamp unto my feet and Light unto my path. And a lighted lamp must be a burning lamp.

Moreover, only Jesus, "that Burning Lamp could pass between those two pieces to THIS Fourth Generation" (Gen 15: 12-16). For those pieces represent Jesus Christ as the Offering for Sin by the Goat for Sin the Lamb who takes away sin, the Ram who atones for Sin in both Sanctuaries, under the Two Prophetic Time Periods:

The 2300 Days of the Earthly   The 1290 Days of the Heavenly
   Sanctuary by {70} Weeks   Sanctuary by 70 years
        Dn 8:13-14)   &   (Dn 12:11-12)

For there is Only One Mediator between a holy God and sinful man, yea and as He is to a people of THIS Generation today; HE was to the generations of old. Yes, Adam My Son! I will cover you, for MY LAMB has been prepared and slain from the foundation of the World; because I knew that you would sin.

Yes, "WOMAN! What have you done?

Now Behold Your Son" (Jn 19:26). For THIS is what you have done. No, He did not say MOTHER, behold your Son, but "woman" for hanging in the balance between Heaven and Earth, looking back down through the corridor of time, the CREATOR Who must also become man's SAVIOR saw only the specimen of the WOMAN, that caused the Transgression: "but she shall be saved in childbearing, if they [the Church], continue in the faith..." (1 Tim 2:13-15). So yes:

Woman! behold your Son.

I have the LAMB Adam, and I will provide the Sacrifice, so that You and your seed will not be cut off from the face of the Earth:

"for HE who keeps the Fig Tree
shall honor his Master" (Pro 27:18)
And in that Day, THE LAST DAYS, it shall come to pass,

> that every man shall sit under his
> own fig tree [with his 200], and none
> shall make him afraid" (Mic 4:1-4)
>
> For "great Peace have they that LOVE thy LAW and
> nothing shall offend them" (Ps 119: 65).
> For "THIS Man" shall be
> our Peace " (Mic 5:5, Eph 2:14).

Therefore, having died to restore and magnify God's Law that Adam had broken initially, which destroyed the Peace between God and man; when Jesus was ready to return to His Father, HE breathe upon His disciples His Peace [God's Peace] again, declaring:

"My Peace I Give unto You,

My Peace I leave with you" (Jn 14:27).

So! sing your Song Solomon. Let's hear it: for "the fig tree hath put forth her green figs, and the vines with the tender grapes give a good smell" (SS 2:13). Oh! But I know that, not ALL will love ME, so the "good figs must be separated from the naughty figs into two basket" (Jer 24:2), as the wheat is separated from the tare; yea the sheep from the goat until I return. Yes, raise your notes in melodious sonnet, Solomon for the Apple Tree represents the LOVE of God, but the Fig Tree, symbolizes the Peace of God, as the First Two Trees of God's Garden. For Love and Peace, breathes Joy. So by one man's disobedience SIN came, even so by ONE shall many be turned unto Righteousness" (Ro 5:19). Adam broke IT but Jesus came and fixed IT

> And Now
>
> Arise my LOVE, my fair one, and come away!

FOR ONE GREATER THAN SOLOMON IS NOW IN THE GARDEN.

CHAPTER FOUR

THE PALM TREE

The first tree in the Midst of God's Garden have been attacked

And God has been defiled by man.

Tree of Knowledge   &   The Tree of Life

{God the Father}   {God the Son—The WORD}

But you will no more defile "the Place of My throne, nor the Sole of My

Feet, where I will dwell

in the Midst of the children of Israel forever" (Ezek 43:7). For God's Place is always in the Midst. "Let them build Me a Sanctuary that I may dwell in the Midst of them" (Ex 28:8).

And so God placed His Two Trees in Eden's Garden Temple,
in the Midst
{symbolically, prophetically and metaphorically representing the Soles of the Feet, of Both Father and Son, standing in the midst}.

The Father by the First Tree, the Tree of knowledge of Good and Evil. Therefore, because the First Tree was touched, it defiled the First Person of the Godhead, causing a "lack of knowledge" (Hos 4:6). So now, "if we desire knowledge, we must ask the Father personally, Who gives it generously" (Jam 1:5).

The Second Tree, the Tree of Life, represented God's Son, the One that was sent, to reconcile and lead us back to the Father. Hence HE declares "I AM the Way, the Truth and the Life" no man comes unto the Father but through ME. So, once man was driven out of the

Garden, God preserve the Tree of Life, so that man cannot find his way back to God but through Jesus Christ. Hence it is written: "and this is Life Eternal, that they may know ME, the ONLY True God, and Jesus Christ, whom I have sent" (Jn 17:3). For the TWO Cherubs on both sides of the Mercy Seat, where God Almighty sits upon His Throne (Ex 25:17-22), represents Jesus Christ facing the Father, Man's Mediator in both Sanctuaries.

Therefore, having defiled the Father, and driven away the Son Joy departed from the House of the Lord. Yes! :

> "be ashamed O ye husbandman, howl O ye
>
> vinedressers, for the wheat and for the barley; because
>
> the harvest of the field is perished. The vine is
>
> dried up, and the fig tree languished, the pomegranate tree,
>
> THE PALM TREE ALSO,
>
> and the apple tree, even all the trees of the
>
> field are withered because
>
> JOY is withered away from the sons of men" (Jl 1:112)

Albeit, HE who said "Let US make man" has also declared: "Man has become as one of US. Let US go down to the Garden and deal with man, lest he put forth his hand and take also of the TREE of Life" (Gen 1:26, 3:22-24):

> Adam! Where art thou?

You must leave My Garden Temple and take everything that belong to you with you, the woman, that you put before ME, for you "have left your first love, and hearkened unto your wife" (Gen 3:17). Remember how you have fallen and repent" (Re 2:4-5).

Get out Adam! get out of My Garden Temple

and go and toil out in the Field.

And of course, the "field is the World" (Mt 13:38). Henceforth, God closed the GATE, of His Temple in the East and placed Cherubs at both sides to keep the Tree of Life. And the Gate was shut and remained shut until Jesus [the Prince] came and died to become the True Temple (Ezek 44:1-4). For the Palm Tree cannot stand without the Two Cherubim. Hence the Cherubim stood to the First Two Parts, and still stands today with the Palm Tree, to the THIRD Part in sequential order in God's Temple in heaven, for the "Earthly Temple was made exactly after the Heavenly" (Heb 8:5); so that when the Earthly was made extinct by the Cross, the Law was ratified by the BLOOD, and the Temple in Heaven was open exposing the LAW of God within the Ark of God (Rev 11:19).

Hence the "Cherubim and Palm Trees were found throughout the Temple (1 Kgs 6:23-32). So that a palm tree was between the two Cherubs and every cherub had two faces. The face of a Man, was toward the Palm Tree on one side and the face of a young Lion is toward the Palm Tree on the other side throughout all the house" (Ezek 41:18-19). Hence the two Sanctuaries, by the Third and Fourth Generations" (Ex 20:5, Num 14:18) under the Two Prophetic Time Periods (Dan 8:13-14, 12: 11-12)

PAST	PRESENT
The Earthly by the	**The Heavenly by the**
2300 Days to the	**1290 Days to the**
First Two Parts of the House	**Third Part of the House,**

Therefore, the face of a man looked FORWARD in time toward the Palm Tree, as the Messiah to come, while the face of a lion looks back in Time to the Palm Tree, as our Lion, of Judah, our Deliverer today, our Reigning High Priest (Heb 8:24-28). For "when the daily sacrifices were taken away" (Dan 12:11) on Calvary, it represented

Jesus as Mediator to the First Two Parts who lived under animal sacrifices:

```
                          Most Holy Place
        Face of a Man as                    Face of Lion as
        Promised Messiah                   as Redeemer and King
      In the Earthly Sanctuary           In the Heavenly Sanctuary
      C         P        Mercy   Seat    P              C
      H         A        _____A              H
      E   looked  L         A R K        L    looks     E
      R   forward M      OF THE COVENANT  M    back      R
      U     to   >       _____<     to       U

      B         T                        T              B
      I         R                        R              I
      M         E                        E              M
                E                        E
    Under the 2300 Days              Under the 1290 Days
     Prophetic Period                  Prophetic Period
      (Dan 8:13-14)                   (Dan 12:6-7, 11-12)
    How Long to Vision of             How Long to the
      daily sacrifice                 Signs & Wonders
                                      looking back to
                                      daily sacrifice.
```
{Jesus the Only Mediator between God and Man}

Wherefore, Jesus stands symbolically by the Two "Cherubs on both sides of the Mercy Seat, as Intercessor on man's behalf, in the Second part, the Holiest {the Temple}. Thus the cherubs which symbolically represented Jesus were made out of the olive tree" (1 Kgs 6:23), also depicting HIM, as The Two "Faithful Witnesses by the Two Olive Trees" (Rev 11:3-12). And these two olive trees can also be found on both sides of the BOWL of the candlestick (Zech 4:1-4), in the Sanctuary, the first part, that is called "the Holy Place" (He 9:2-3). Cherubim and Palm Trees stand together symbolically as Father and Son, Past, Present and Future. For "I and My Father are One" inseparable. "I in the Father and the Father dwelling in Me "(Jn 14:10-11). Therefore, after Sin appeared, God barred up His Garden Temple and placed Cherubim to keep the Tree of Life, thus implementing the Sanctuary as a result of SIN. And all flesh are Beneficiaries of the Sanctuary, past and present, for all have sinned" (Ro 3:23).

And so! Coming out of Egypt, after the Great Deluge of the First and Second Generations, it was time once again, for GOD to introduce HIMSELF to His people of the Third and Fourth Generations: declaring "let them make ME a Sanctuary, that I may dwell in the **Midst** of them" (Ex 25:8-22), just as the Two Trees stood in the **Midst** for God's Place is always in the Midst of His people, hence "the Sanctuary in the **Midst**" (Ezek 48:8,10,21,35). For "thy Way O God is in the Sanctuary"(Ps 77:13). Hence the Cherubim, yea the Sanctuary that was closed up in Eden was again given to the Third and Fourth Generations with the "MERCY SEAT between the Two Cherubs". For I, the Most High dwell between the Cherubim" and where the Cherubim are the Palm Tree will always be (Ezek 41:17-25). For that which started in Eden when it was Lost to man, will be given back to man when Eden is RESTORED, at the "End of the 1335 Days" (Dan 12:12).

And so Solomon sang in melodious sonnet

of the STATURE of the Palm Tree" (SS 7:7-8), for thus says

the Almighty "be ye Holy, for I am holy" (Lev 11:45),

"flourishing like the Palm tree" (Ps 92:13-15). A statue

all heaven bound pilgrims must attain through

Jesus Christ, Man's Mediator, symbolic of the

Cherubim; before the Cross and today, after the Cross, for

HE is the Only Savior of the World.

So one cherub looked forward in Time Past, while the other cherub looks back in Present Time to the Palm Tree today, a symbol of

Jesus standing before the Most High God, seated upon His Mercy Seat; as man's Mediator and Intercessor in the Heavenly Sanctuary. The Palm Tree is the most Stately Tree of all the land, symbolically representing God Almighty. Hence the Seventy palm trees, the city of palm trees where, weary travelers found refuge and lodging (Jud 1:16). Yea! even the Prophetess Deborah sat metaphorically under the Palm Tree as She ruled Israel. And Barak, knew that he could follow a woman who followed after; and surrendered herself unto God, in judging the people of God (Jud 4:5).

Nevertheless, it is not over with the Palm Tree, until it is all over. For as those two nations {Jews and Gentiles} applauded the Messiah, "HOSANNAH" spreading down palm branches for Him to ride upon, during His triumphant entry (Jn 12:13), even so will the "AFTER" group of (Rev 7:9-14) from the Third Part of the House of Jacob, {our Prophetic Father}, our World today, stand in our lot upon the Sea of Glass to applaud and reverence, our Leader and Commander giving homage to the LAMB.

Yes! the redeemed, will come forth from every Nation, kindred, tongue and people, clad in robes of white, wearing crowns of Victory, and bearing PALMS of Glory in their hands as they stand before the Lamb" (Rev 7:9). Each with the "ensigns of their Father's House" (Num 2:2), their own national flag color; in a kaleidoscope of nations, "a multitude, that no man can number". Hence the Coat of many Colors that Jacob give unto Joseph, His Son, represents the nations of the redeemed, of the Lord, through the prophetic holdings of the Divine Order. For:

"Thou has with thy arm, redeemed thy people, the sons of

Jacob and Joseph" (Ps 77:15)

No! the Coat was not given, neither was the "crossing of Jacob's hand" because of Joseph or a rejection of Manasseh as the first born of His beloved Rachel, his favorite, as finite minds might suggests, but because it was appointed that Jesus, the Shepherd of Israel would come through Joseph's Camp: "from thence is the Shepherd, the Stone of Israel" (Gen 49:22-24). Wherefore, no part of God's Word stands alone, by the dictates or actions of man, but every dot, tittle and age number given:

like Abraham being called at 75 yrs: and the {1335} Days (Dan 12: 11-12), of the Sanctuary, all projected God's Salvation in the Sanctuary. So it was Divinely appointed that Ephraim was chosen as Head of Samaria {Gentiles} (Is 7:9), as Jacob was born to rule in preference over Esau "the younger . . ." (Gen 25:23). Moreover, that which began with Abraham at 75 years will climax with the {1335} days.

For {1335 - 75 = 1260}, gives God's prophetic number, as HIS Sign to HIS Three Part House in the Earth by the prophetic "woman" of {1260} days. For that which began with Abraham at 75 years will end in Jesus with the {1335} Days at the End of the World. And today, Jesus is God's prophetic SIGN to His Remnant Church, by the "Prophetic Woman of 1260 day" (Rev 12:6,14, 17). For Jesus declared*

JESUS   **ABRAHAM**

1260 < *"before Abraham was I AM"(Jn 8:58) > 75 yrs

because every Word is connected by Divine Providence, to fulfill God's Purpose through Prophecy. And out of Joseph's Camp, through Ephraim, the Gentiles became a people of God, and today we are of "the Remnant of Jacob, among the Gentiles"(Mic 5:8) having come out of the Gentiles, even as the Gentiles came out of the Jews, but all things of God. Moreover, Jacob' our Prophetic Father was not speaking for the benefit of his biological sons, when he gave his Last Will and Testimony, because they are not alive to see these LAST DAYS, of the Prophecy today:

"gather yourselves together, that I may tell you what

shall befall you in the LAST DAYS" (Gen 49:1). No! Jacob's

biological sons are not, but we his spiritual
Sons and daughters are.

OH! What a glorious sight to behold on that Day

Just imagine it, as the Lamb's Bride stand before the Father adorned in the "righteous white linen" (Rev 19:8) of Her Beloved. Well! what do you have here MY Son. "What {who} are these, and where did they come from" (Rev 7:13-14)

Oh My Father! "SIR thou knows".

these are they who have come out of MY tribulation.

And there was never any tribulation like IT,
before NEITHER after

since man was upon the face of the earth" (Mt 24:21, 29).

So man deserves the wages of Sin, now and always, and there will be no tribulation to great ahead for them. BUT! the Righteous Son of God did not deserve Sin's wages, hence HIS Tribulation. The cruel, ignominious, horrifying and shameful execution of the Righteous Son of God? Oh! but My Blood Father, this Third Part have been washed in MY BLOOD, not the blood of goats and bulls, as the first two parts, of the Houses of Abraham and Isaac, from the East and West, but from Jacob, of the "Nations down in the Valley" (Jl 3:1-2). And yes, there will be peace in the valley some day. Hence JESUS declared, when you get to heaven you will sit down in One of THREE groups: "I say unto you, many shall come from the East and West, and shall sit down with Abraham, Isaac and Jacob in the Kingdom of Heaven" (Mt 8:11).

And now My Father, here is My Bride, Your Daughter {Zion}.

Oh yes! Let us be glad and rejoice for the Marriage

of the Lamb is come and His Wife hath made

herself ready" (Rev 19:8-9); as

the Redeemed, adorned in white Robes, with starry Crowns upon their heads and PALM wreaths of Victory in their hands to lay before the LAMB, their Redeemer, in the midst of the THRONE. Yes the Palm Tree will provide palm wreaths of victory for the Redeemed. So! let the Song of triumph ring for they have come out of great tribulation, with much anticipation into great Jubilation, standing gloriously and majestically adorned in celestial strains, before the LAMB.

HERE STANDS THE BRIDE, THE LAMB'S WIFE!

Can you See YOURSELF by Faith standing with your Palm wreath in hand to lay it down for the INARGUATION OF HIS Royal Majesty, Jesus, just as the First Two Parts spread their palm branches down for Jesus, Hosanna!

Our LAMB! KINGS OF KINGS AND LORD OF LORDS?

Reservation has been reserved, with an inheritance made JUST for

Y O U! Be there.

CHAPTER FIVE

THE POMEGRANATE TREE

The Pomegranate Tree stands next in

Sequence, coming behind the Palm Tree, and

symbolically depicting Jesus Christ, as

Savior of the World. For man needed a Mediator and

no man can come back unto the Father but through the SON.

The pomegranate is a round-shaped maroon fruit with a spur like crown, a rosette at the top depicting the Crown of Thorns upon the head of the dying Lamb of God. Inside of the pomegranate are a multiple of tiny seeds, filled with blood-like juice press together in the rind, depicting what the members of the Body of Christ, should be like in the Unity of the Faith. The pomegranate is One of the Three fruits of Salvation, brought back upon a staff by the two spies, depicting Jesus between the two thieves hanging on the Cross. And oh! the depth of His descent.

The pomegranate was also found throughout the Temple, projecting the Messiah, as the Savior to come: "he made the pillars, and two rows to cover the pillars with pomegranates " (1 Kgs 7:18-20) The pomegranate was a definite MUST, a Command that adorned the Priest's Garment, as representatives of Christ:

"a golden bell and a pomegranate, upon

the hem of the robe made of

Blue, Purple and Scarlet" (Ex 28:31-35).

And if the instructions were not followed and obeyed, the priest would be pulled out dead. For all who represented Jesus before the Mercy Seat in the Presence of the Most High God, had to be covered by the pomegranate, as a precautionary measure of righteousness and total obedience. But the pomegranate was not ONLY one of the THREE Fruits of Salvation, it was also made of the THREE Colors of Salvation:

> BLUE: depicting Jesus as the Obedient Son
>
> of God, hence a blue ribbon to
>
> help them {the Church} to "remember" (Num 15:38-39)
>
> PURPLE : depicts Jesus' Royalty, as King of Kings
>
> SCARLET: depicts His Blood: for though your sins be
>
> as scarlet, I will make them as snow.

Therefore, during Jesus' anguish, they placed the purple and scarlet robes upon the Obedient Body of the Son of God (Mk 15:20, Mt 27:28); symbolically mocking Him as King of the Jews. Moreover, Jesus was also projected, prophetically as the Messiah to come by the THREE colors of the Wilderness Tabernacle:

> BLUE - PURPLE - SCARLET.

For the Wilderness Tabernacle, was made out of BLUE, PURPLE and SCARLET; and so were the pomegranates, with emphasis on the Veil and the door (Ex 26:1, 31, 36), all depicting Jesus Christ as:

> 1. The True Temple Tabernacle (Ex 26:1, Rev 21:1-3, 22)
>
> 2. Mediator by the curtain that hung between as the
>
> Veil, His Flesh—(Ex 26:31, Heb 10:21).
>
> 3. And by the Door—I Am the Door (Ex 26:36, Jn 10:7-9).

Henceforth, anything that represented the Person of Jesus Christ in the Temple was made of the Blue, Purple and Scarlet, for He is the True Temple. Therefore, the pomegranate with the fig, and grape are fitting symbols of Jesus, as the Healer of Galilee. For as the fig was used in Hezekiah's recovery (Is 38:21), it is also said that the pomegranate aided in early Bible times, as a cure for Dysentery, a disease of the bowels. The fruit of the pomegranate also makes a peculiar syrup called Grenadine, the confectioner's choice for a treat

Yes Solomon! raise your sound to the melody of the

Pomegranate, for

"thy temples are like a piece of pomegranate" (SS 4:3)

So "I went down into my Garden, to see if

the pomegranate budded"

Is there any wonder why Jesus spend the whole night in the Garden, praying until His sweat became as drops of blood? But knowing who He was, and what He knew, Solomon narrated "with all the trees of frankincense; myrrh and aloes, and all the chief spices" (SS 4:14), that would be used in His Death and Burial? A "mixture of myrrh and aloes, with the spice . . . thus fulfilling the prophecy. For in the place where He was crucified, there was a Garden; and in the Garden, a new sepulcher." (Jn 19:39-41). No! it was not by chance that the Garden was near the sepulcher, but by purpose and design in the Prophetic Holdings of Salvation. Yes! My Beloved is gone down into His Garden {to the sleep of death}, to His bed of spices

For my Beloved is mine, and I am my Beloved's (SS 6:2-3).

Come! Into the Garden

FOR THERE WILL I GIVE THEE MY LOVE (SS 6:11, 7:12)

CHAPTER SIX

THE CLUSTERS OF GRAPES

He broke the Law {Apple Tree}, destroyed his

Peace {Fig Tree}, and drove away

the Most High {the Palm Tree} necessitating

a Savior {the Pomegranate Tree}.

And now blood must be shed. So! come down into My Garden, and see "the tender grapes appear" as the Grape Vine followed the pomegranate in God's Garden representing the Blood of the LAMB of God, that flowed forth from His Head, His Hands, Feet and Side to bring about that fountain for Sin's cleansing. For as the pomegranate depicts Him as Savior, the grape depicts his blood, and the barley his flesh:

For flesh + blood = man.

Yes He was a Man of Sorrow and acquainted with grief. Wounded, smitten of God and numbered with the transgressors (Is 53:3-12). Hence the GRAPE also stood with the POMEGRANATE and FIG (Num 13:20-23) symbolically representing Jesus between the two spies:

Jerusalem		Samaria
Caleb of Judah	(Num 13:6-8)	Osehea {Ephraim}

even as He hung between the two thieves

upon a wooden cross as "The first fruit of the land,

for it was the time of the first ripe grapes".

All because the Omnipotent God had His Plan purposely fixed within the Prophetic holdings of Salvation, distinguishing Jesus Christ; from the Thedus(s) and Judas(s) of this world (Acts 5:35-39) who paraded around as "somebody." But "This Same Jesus" (Acts 1:11), oh yes He is SOMEBODY, for no other can fit into the prophetic mold of the THREE fruits by the THREE colors of Salvation.

Therefore, while the Pomegranate depicts HIM—As Savior, the Grape, "the first ripe grape" symbolizes His Blood; and the Fig depicts Him as the Prince of Peace: for "He is our Peace" (Eph 2:14) yet they did not know Him, accusing Him as an imposter, who claimed that he was the Son of God. Crucify Him, yes that was the Church sanctioning His Death:

> Yea! "I had planted them a noble vine, wholly a
>
> Right Seed. How art thou turned into a
>
> degenerate Plant of a strange vine unto Me"? (Je 2:21)

Well! "woe is ME: for I am as when they have the summer fruits; as the grape-gleanings of the vintage. And there is no cluster to eat? Oh! How My Soul desired, the clusters. So the good man is perished out of the Earth and there is none Upright" (Mi 7:2). And also with the Good Man, the harvest of the field had perished, and the Vine was dried up" (Jl 1:11-12).

What! No clusters? Oh the clusters!

Well, we are no different today for we love to eat the clusters too, then we cast the vine into the waste for the fire. Even so will "God cast the vine into the winepress of His Wrath". Then the Holy Ghost, who has Power over Fire, will give the last loud cry, for the harvest of God will be reaped by the ANGELS: Spirit Beings, comprising God the Father, Jesus the Son of Man [Michael, the Archangel] with the Sharp Sickle in His Hand and God, the Holy Ghost, as They "come out of the Temple of Heaven" (Rev 14:14-20).]

> So give ME some clusters; for clusters represents
>
> the righteous children of God.

Thy two breast are to me as roes that are twins; as clusters" (SS 4:5, 7:7) and twins prophetically they were, as Joint Heirs together, God's "Two Prophetic Daughters" (Ezek 23:1-4). Ahola and Aholabah, daughters of One Woman {God's Church} depicted by Two Breasts as clusters:

One Prophetic Woman with Two Daughters As Two Breasts

{Aholibah} Jerusalem	C	Samaria {Aholah}
	A	
3 ½ days	L	3 ½ days
prophetic years	V	of prophetic years
Caleb of Judah	A	Oshea {Joshua} Ephraim(Is 7:9)
Two spies depicts >	R <	the two thieves
{Ezek 23:1-4	Y	{One Woman's children}

There I lie betwixt thy Two breast "A bundle of myrrh is my well-beloved unto me; he shall lie all night betwixt my breasts" sleeping in the darkness of Death, as HE was "Cut-off in the Midst" (SS 1:13, Dan 9:27) between the Two nations of Israel, simultaneously "cutting off the Two Parts" (Zec 13:8-9)

"Thou art beautiful My Love, as Tirzah and

Comely as Jerusalem" (SS 6:4)

Where HE hung in the Midst, between the Two

in the Night season to bring an End to the blood of animal sacrifices. And so, before making His way to Golgotha to drink that bitter Cup of {Myrrh} and to be embalmed with Aloes (SS 4:14); from His Garden, My Beloved celebrated His Last Supper:

> Yes bring forth the clusters, for unless YOU

> Eat My flesh and drink My Blood

You can have no part with ME. But "as often as you do this, do it in remembrance of Me. For I shall no more drink of this Fruit with you, until I drink it anew in My Father's Kingdom" (Lk 22:15-20). Thus HE has left His Beloved His Dying Promise:

> For lo! I will return for the Clusters:

> "thrust in thy Sickle and reap"

For there must be clusters to eat. Oh "how fair and how pleasant art thou O Love for delights for this thy Statue is like to a palm tree and thy two breasts to clusters of Grapes" (SS 7:6-8) as Jerusalem and Samaria. Oh! but there will also be a reaping of clusters from the Third Part, the House of Jacob, the infant Church of God:

> For although "Our Little Sister does not

> have any breast yet, she has been spoken for"

And She will be perfected at His Coming, as HE comes to deal with the Third Part of men" (Rev 9:14-15). So "thrust in thy Sickle and reap and gather the Clusters of the Vine, for her grapes are ripe" (Rev 14:14-18). Albeit, the clusters of the grapes are all alike joined together on the vine, just as all the seeds of the pomegranate are pressed together within the rind, depicting unity in the Body of Christ. And now, for the BIG question:

> Who do you want to reign over YOU?

"The trees said to the Olive Tree [Jesus], reign over us. But shall I leave my fatness wherewith they honor God and man to reign over you"? I stand in high places as Cherubs with the Most High, at the Mercy Seat.

> "Then the trees called for the Fig Tree

To Reign over them. Now! Shall I leave my sweetness, my good fruit"{the Peace of God} to reign over you"?

"So the trees asked the Vine

Will you Reign over us? How shall I leave my wine which cheers God and man. For promotion to Reign over you".

"Then the trees said to the Bramble

Come thou and reign over us, and the Bramble [Satan] said: if in TRUTH, you anoint me, and put your trust in me I will, and if not ; let fire come out of the bramble and devour all the trees of Lebanon.

Oh the Trees! the trees, for in God's Garden,

all flesh are symbolically regarded prophetically as trees. Either you are a green tree as "trees of righteousness" (Is 61:3, Ps 52:8); or a dry tree (Is 56:3), to be cast into the fire. Hence Jotham's Parable (Jud 9:8-15). The choice is ours, but the Olive tree [Jesus], knows His Place beside the Father, and the Fig tree loves its Peace and communion with God. The Grape vine refuses to reign because the BLOOD which still *prevails*, cannot cover anything, that *curtails* the WORD. So we must first be washed by the WORD of TRUTH (Jn 15:3, Eph 5:26), in order to be covered by the Blood of the FRUIT {blessed is the Fruit of thy womb}. OR that certain woman {the Lamb's Wife}, that strong tower, the Church Of the Living God, will drop Judgment upon the head, at that day(Jud 9:51-53), that not even death will be able to deliver us.

So! which will you be

Cluster or Vine? Yea! My beloved loves to eat the clusters.

For "a bundle of myrrh is my well beloved unto Me; and he shall lie All night betwixt my breast" (SS 1:13-14). Albeit, between the breasts of man {woman} lies the organ of the heart, which causes the BLOOD to circulate. And as long as the blood circulates, you are ALIVE and can PRAISE God with your whole heart. The heart is the seat of our affections and emotions, the central part of man's existence.

So! give ME your heart, let ME lie between your breasts.

Let Me break your heart "for a broken and a contrite heart, I will not despise"(Ps 51:17) then I will take away your stony heart and give you a new heart a heart of flesh" (Ezek 11:18-20).

FOR

MY BELOVED IS MINE AND I AM HIS

CHAPTER SEVEN

THE BARLEY GRAIN

The "Appointed Barley and the Principle Wheat"

(Is 28:25)

The body consists of flesh and blood, henceforth as the Grape is to the blood, so is the Barley to the flesh, symbolically representing the Son of Man as the First Fruit of the Spiritual Harvest. Yea, of them that slept. For Barley and Wheat belong together as God and man who was created in His image. Hence the God-man, the Son of God.

Listen as He speaks of His Beloved, His Woman

"go love a woman according to the LOVE of

the Lord. I purchased Her for fifteen pieces of silver and

fifteen homers of barley. YOU shall abide for ME, many

days {prophetic years}

YOU must not be for another Man,
and I will be only for thee" (Hos 3:1-4)

Fifteen and fifteen makes Thirty {15 + 15 = 30}

for both barley and Silver symbolically represents the Body of Christ. The Barley as the Son of God; and the silver as the Son of Man. However, while ALL flesh is symbolically represented as silver, only the United THREE of the Godhead can be metaphorically and significantly regarded as barley, hence the "THREE measures of Barley to One measure of Wheat" (Rev 6:6), Y O U! Wherefore to have Jesus Christ, to love and honor Him, is to have God the Father and Obey Him by the indwelling Power of the Holy

Spirit whose Temple Y O U are" (1 Co 6:19). Silver on the other hand, metaphorically depicts all flesh. Hence the Silver Part of the Breasts and Arms of the Four Part Prophetic Beast prophetically depicting, the Age of the CHURCH of God in the Earth; as GOLD is to the WORLD.

And today the House of God, stand prophetically in the Earth; decreed by the THREE earthly kings of the Silver age of Medes and Persia (Dan 2: 38-44, Ezra 6:1-15). For the Church was build and restored during the Kingdoms of this dual Entity: Medes and Persia according to the Divine Plan. Hence The WORD declared of Jesus in the Sanctuary: "the Prince of Persia withstood ME"(Dan 10:13).

GOLD	SILVER	BRASS	IRON/CLAY
The World	The Church	The People	The Savior
Dan 2:38	Ezra 6:3-16	Ex 32:9, Is 48:4	Jer 15:12

And so, the thirty pieces of Silver, in weight and cost complements both the barley and silver as the Offering of Christ:

> "15 pieces of silver and 15 homers of barley"
>
> they weighed for my price, thirty
>
> pieces of Silver" (Zech 11:12).

And all flesh share in this allegory as Silver, for either you are "reprobate silver" (Je 6:30, Ro 1:28; 2 Tim 3:8, 1 Co 13:5-7), or You are "refined Silver" (Zech 13:9). But one way or another you are prophetically regarded as Silver. Hence the Woman, the Church was purchased for {15 pieces of silver and 15 homers of barley} depicting the body of Jesus Christ.

> Moreover, the "Appointed Barley" is to Christ
>
> as the Principal Wheat is to humanity" (Is 28:25).

For humanity is the Sum total of Jesus' Death on Calvary. So gather the wheat in My Barn" (Mt 3:12). For as "the flax and the barley were smitten"; even so was Christ "smitten" (Is 53:4). But the wheat and rye were not smitten, because they had not grown up yet" to reach maturity as the Barley and the Flax (Ex 9:32-32), by Jesus our Elder Brother. Yes! Jesus matured first, reaching immortality, as the "First Fruit of {the Barley Harvest}, of them that slept" (1 Co 15:20). Nevertheless, "we too shall be like a kind of first fruit" (Jam 1:18); like Jesus, when we are changed and immortalized at His Coming.

The barley cakes principally were to service

The men of God" (2 Kgs 4:42)

Hence the Six measures of barley given in the veil (Ru 3:15) prophetically represented Jesus, the WORD, {our kinsman Redeemer} carried by the Six men, that stood with HIM, Man "Number Seven, clothed in Linen" (Ezek 9:2-11) even as "the Seven shepherds" (Mi 5:5), stood before the Most High God, at the Higher Gate, and as the Candlestick with the SIX Branches: THREE branches on one side; and THREE branches on the other side {3+3=6}; with the Silver Bowl at the top borne by the Man in the midst. And in that Silver Bowl are all the confessed sins, of all people of all the ages, borne by Jesus Christ, the Man in the midst of the Candlestick as the only Savior:

THE HIGHER GATE

1st Generation	F	3rd Generation
Adam	L	Abraham
Seth	O	Isaac
2ND Generation Noah	O	Jacob
	D	

JESUS   Our 4th Generation Head

"This Man shall be our Peace"(Mi 5:5)

And HE "cut of the three shepherds in one month" (Zech 11:8) that stood before Him{Abraham, Isaac, Jacob} on this Side of the Flood, to bring home the trophy as SAVIOR. Hence the {7}Churches by the {7}Candlestick, represents Jesus Christ Man #7, the WORD as the STAR, carried by the Six Men, as Leaders over God's flock in the earth, before Bethlehem Star made His entrance among the cattle of the manger stall. For both the Barley and the Veil depicts the Body of Christ. Albeit! the moral of 'from rags to riches' truly befits Ruth the Moabite, the gleaner, who received the Six measures of barley in the Veil; as she rose to Heaven's Hall of Fame, "be thou famous in Bethlehem" (Ru 4:11); to stand as MOTHER of Zion, in High Places, with Leah and Rachael at the Gate.

Oh! but did you see the destruction that the Barley caused to the Camp of Middian (Jug 7:13) because of whom it represents? So, I have purchased YOU with Barley and Silver, making You Mine. Hence the Lord's Supper.

For as You EAT my flesh and DRINK My Blood you honor ME:

$$BLOOD + FLESH = MAN$$

$$\{Grape\} \quad \{Barley\}$$

And so significantly, the {Grape of the Vine followed by the Barley of the Corn} represent Jesus Christ, Past, Present and Future as Savior

And His Banner over Us is

L O V E

CHAPTER EIGHT

MANDRAKES

In Song and Sonnet, the wise man told us of

"Fruits New and Old" (SS 7:13).

And that is how God works, by the Old and the New, as His Two Faithful Witnesses, the WORD. The mandrake is an old fruit, not common to our world today. Nevertheless, it is used prophetically to describe the sweet smelling scent at the Gate of the Lord's House. The mandrake is a fruit, of the plant from the Potato family. It grows very low to the ground, with large, dark green leaves, spreading out like a circle. And from the center of the circle, the flower stalks grow, each bearing only one whitish-blue looking flower that gives a purple look at Bloom. The fruit from the plant grows to the size of a Plum that ripens to a red color during the wheat harvest:

"and Ruben went in the days of the wheat harvest,

and found mandrakes in the field and

brought them to his mother Leah. Then Rachael

said to Leah give me, I pray thee,

of thy son's mandrakes" (Gen 30:14).

The mandrake which was said to have the resemblance of a man's lower limb, gave a positive view that it aided in infertility; and Rachael who was barren, wanted children more than anything else. Hence the quarrel between the Two Sisters, {Jerusalem and Samaria}:

"Is it a small matter that thou has taken my husband

and you want to take my son's mandrakes also"?

Rachael envied her sister, and said unto Jacob, HER Husband

"GIVE ME CHILDREN, OR I DIE"

Am I in God's stead" (Gen 30:1-2)

Therefore, Rachael said unto Leah "He can lie with You tonight for thy son's mandrakes" (Gen 30:15-24). Yes! Leah received her hire, Issachar

B U T!

Rachael got the better part, for her Faith worked and she "*prevailed*" (Gen 30:8), as *all* Over-comers must prevail. Albeit, Jacob also wrestle and prevailed, but Leah did not. Hence the True Wife, Rachael the Shepherdess of Israel was; not only one to wrestle but She also prevailed, (Gen 35:16). And as the Mother of the Covenant, of the House of Jacob She died in Her *Travail,* in the wake of birthing Zion. Laying down her life in Bethlehem, in the very same place, where Jesus, our Spiritual Father who also "*prevailed*" to reign over Jacob's House began His Life. For Jacob could not and did not *travail* and as Head of the House to the Remnant; one must not only *prevail*, but also *travail*. Therefore, reigning over Jacob's House (Lk 1:33), Jesus like Rachael travailed for us: "***travailing*** to bring forth His Woman His

Church, His Beloved. Hence the structure of :

JACOB'S HOUSE, THE HOUSE OF GOD (Is 2:2-3)

Jacob	Rachael	Jesus
Our Prophetic Father	Our Prophetic Mother	Our Spiritual Father
Prevailed Only	prevailed & travailed *	prevailed & travailed*

Yes! a woman shall compass a man" (Je 31:22). And Rachael compassed Jacob, travailing where he could not. And "God remembered Rachael and opened her womb, taking away her reproach". Henceforth, through the descendant of Rachael was the Covenant maintained, as Joseph and Ephraim, championed the Course, allowing for Jesus, the Stone of Israel to make His Way into Samaria:

> **"I have a need to go into Samaria"**
>
> **to the Well" (Gen 49:22-24, Jn 4: 5-6).**

Mandrakes therefore symbolically represents the children of the Covenant, God's people in His Garden. They give off a sweet smelling aroma at the Gate of the Lord's House" (SS 7:13). So "enter into His Gates with thanksgiving, and come into His Courts with praise" (Ps 100:4). The Gate: "Oh how dreadful is THIS PLACE, this is none other than House of God and the Gate to Heaven" hence the people of God give a pleasant scent in the nostrils of the "God of Jacob at the Gate of the House of the God of Jacob"(Is 2:2-3) Z I O N.

"And God loves Zion more than all the dwellings of Jacob" Ps 87:1

Mandrakes, like the pomegranates and figs also had healing properties in early Bible days, for it is said to have been used in preparation as a narcotic for antispasmodic remedies, thus befitting Jesus, the Great Healer. Albeit, all of the trees in God's Garden Temple, promotes health and healing to mankind, physically and spiritually.

No it was not a "light matter" at all that Rachael desired the Mandrakes, for as Mother of the Covenant, She was the rightful Wife of her Beloved, and She died in the crucible, to pay sins price prophetically, as She laid down her life in the wake of birthing ZION, spiritually. Thus "She was buried in the WAY" (Gen 35:15-20). In the Way, "this is the Way, walk ye in it" (Is 30:21).

> For the Lord loves ZION, more than
>
> all the dwellings of Jacob" (Ps 87:1-2)
>
> 'ZION! CITY OF OUR GOD'

CHAPTER NINE

NUTS AND CHIEF SPICES

In the Song of Solomon, much is said about the precious trees in the Garden of the Lord, even as the legacy of the Church Of God today, a watered Garden (Je 31:10-12). For the LORD, God brought thee into a good land, a land of brooks and of springs and fountains out of hills and valleys, a land of wheat and barley and vines, figs and pomegranates a land of oils, of olives and honey, where you can eat bread without scarceness, or lack" (Num 20:5, Dt 8:7-8). Nevertheless, today these precious gifts have lost their significance and appeal to the Church of God, simply because we have lost the significance of the Truth of God hidden in and among the chronicles of prophecy.

Hence Jesus' admonition to *all* is to

"search the Scriptures . . . for they testify

of ME" (Jn 5:39); and if you would know me,

learn of Me in the Psalms and Prophets . . . ME" (Lk 24:44,47)

Many today gloss over Solomon's Songs as a good piece of poetry, that excites the sexual appetite of mankind, yea even of the Old Monarch, the Poet Himself, with his {700 + 300 =1000} women, more than the years of his life:

BUT

"One greater than Solomon is here" (Mt 12:42), *today* and His Love Banner over his people is solid Truth. For HE owns the Gardens From "the Garden of Cedron where HE often resorted (Jn 18:1-2); on to His anguish in the Garden of Gethsemane, ending His mission at Calvary, where they brought a mixture of myrrh and aloes with the Spices. And there in the Garden, they laid Him in a new and borrowed tomb" (Jn 19:39-41).

Well, why would HE need to own a tomb,

since He did not see corruption, as all other flesh

which necessitates such a holding cell of their own.

Therefore, while Solomon sang about them (SS 5:13-15), he could not lay claim to the chief spices with the frankincense, myrrh, and aloes". For they belonged to One greater: JESUS, Rose of Sharon Who spreads His Banner of Love over His people, not Solomon. But Solomon's emotions were aroused to a thrilling sensation, stimulated by the wisdom and understanding of God, that caused him to personalized the ROMANTIC FLARE, of the love and affections of Christ to His Church. Albeit though, the things of God is foolishness to man, because of the "lack of Knowledge" (Ho 4:6); the good Knowledge is often hidden. For there were two kinds of Knowledge depicted on the Tree, that man ate from, "the Tree of Knowledge of Good and Evil" (Gen2:9). And, because man obtained their knowledge by default, humanity craves after the evil side of knowledge, which is man's wisdom. But when we enter into The Sanctuary, as David did" (Ps 73:17), then we too will begin to understand the DEEP things of God and appreciate the wisdom of Solomon; as he narrated romantically Of the World's Greatest Lover. The One who has proven His Love beyond all measure as

> HE laid down his Life for His Woman,
> His Church, His Body, **Y O U!**

The nuts and spices, what are they and what was Solomon so excited about? No, not the peanuts and chestnuts of man's wisdom today; but nuts and almonds from a forever budding tree (Num 17:5-10) the décor of the Candlestick (Ex 25:31-35) and its sweet smelling flowers that adorned; and perpetuated the fragrance of His Temple Presence in the Sanctuary. Yes "what do you see? I see a rod of an almond tree" (Je 1:11). And where was that rod of the almond tree but within the Ark of the Temple. Thus the WORD declares, that they are the best Gifts of the Land:

> "take the best fruits of the land in your vessel

> And carry the Man a Present, a little
>
> balm, honey, spices, myrrh, nuts and almonds"
>
> (Gen 43:11, 37:25)

So "I went down into the garden of nuts, to see fruits of the valley and to see whether the vine flourished and the pomegranate budded" (SS 6:11); and there will I give thee my Love" (SS 7:12). Henceforth, the nuts and chief spices, depicts Jesus Christ, in His Death and burial as the Only Savior. And no! He did not need the "oil of apothecary", as the other high priests had to use (Ex 30:24-25), for His garment smelled of the Cassia and Myrrh, the perfume of His Own Body" (Ps 45:8).

> Oh! "My Dove, My undefiled is but One,
> the only one of her mother,
> {not part of the prophetic twins}; she is the

choice One of her that bare her. Hence the Body of Christ, His Wife is making herself ready, His Bride: the Remnant Church of God, for whom He is coming again. Fairer and more beautiful than the Shulamite, of Solomon's Day; She has Beauty and Perfection and She has been spoken for indeed and favored in His eyes" (SS 8:8-10). A woman sought after, by Her Beloved. Who is she that looks forth as the morning, but the Bride of Christ clothed in the White Linen, of HIS Righteousness (Rev 19:8)

> HIS BELOVED, THE FAIREST AMONG WOMEN. Y o u!

CHAPTER TEN

OUR LITTLE SISTER WITHOUT BREAST

The "Two Prophetic daughters of God

From One Woman,

Aholah and Aholabah and! THESE ARE MINE" (Ezek 23:1-4)

They can never be separated for they have been bounded together as "Joint Heirs" (Eph 3:6) by the Cross. These are the Two Prophetic Twins, with "Two sets of breasts as clusters of grapes" (SS 4:5). Sounds sensual, absolutely not, for God created them both; the female with breast for the male, and God regards Zion [His Church] as a "delicate and comely woman" (Je 2:6). Oh yes those two breast are like clusters of grapes, representing the First Two Parts of God's House in the Earth, that has been "cut-of" (Zech 13:8-9); Samaria [Ahola] the eldest and her little sister Jerusalem [Aholabah], leaving the Third Part, "our little sister" the Infant Church of Christ without breast. And for each of the THREE Part House of God, there was an Offering made in the Sanctuary by THIRTY [30].

The Offering for the First Two Parts of the House, depicted by the TWO women [Joint Heirs together] Jerusalem and Samaria with breasts as clusters were, THIRTY {30 + 30} making {60} goats, lambs and rams each, as the Offering of the Sanctuary (Num 7:88). Thus God's Prophetic Number as His Sign by {60+60+60=180 x 7=**1260**} was established to His THREE Part House in all the Earth by Jesus Christ, Man #7, as the Savior of the World.

Hence God's Sign was to the first Two Parts as {1260} in the dispensations of the Jews and Gentiles, with flocks, and goats, nuts and spices, frankincense and myrrh, pomegranates, barley cakes, mandrakes, and all the trees of the Garden, during the Earthly Sanctuary which is PAST:

First Part	C	Second Part
Jews of 3 ½ Years	R	Gentiles of 42 months
{360+360+360+180= 1260}*	O	{12+12+12+6 = 1260}*
(Rev 11:1)	S	(Rev 11:2)
	S	

Therefore, it must be understood that ALL scripture is given by inspiration of God and is profitable for doctrine, for reproof, for correction, for instruction in righteousness" (2 Ti 3:16-17). Nevertheless, Scripture must be rightly divided (2 Tim 2:15) to each of the THREE Part House of God (Zech 13:8-9). For that which was relevant to the First Two Parts of the House, by the Two women with their two breasts, is not relevant to "Our little sister without breast" (SS 8:8-10) today, thus we must be

"established in PRESENT TRUTH" (2 Pe 1:12)

And Present Truth is, that our little sister also made an Offering by THIRTY. No not as the Jews and Gentiles, by {30 + 30=60}, Sixty goats, lambs and rams (Num 7:88); under the 2300 Days of the Earthly Sanctuary, but by THIRTY pieces of silver {30}, under the 1290 Days of the Heavenly Sanctuary. For the offering for each of the THREE Part House was Thirty{30}.

An so equal time is being served for the Third Part, the Remnant today. No not of 3½ years to the Jews, or of 42 months to the Gentiles (Rev 11:2), but of time, times and half time, to give our{1260} days for the Remnant Church of our end time Generation" (Rev 12:6,14,17). For

Jesus, by God's Sign of {1260}, gave unto each of the THREE parts equal time:

With the Jews	To the Gentiles	For the Remnant
Jesus lived for 3½ yrs* {360+360+360+180= 1260},	He gave 42 months 12+12+12+6= 1260} Rev 11:2	He is serving time, times, & ½ times, {1+2 + 6 months = 3 ½* 1260}

And today Jesus is still serving our little sister without breast, our World today His "Woman of 1260 days" that is *still* hiding in the wilderness for time, times and half time, or 1260 days" (Rev 12:6,14,17) until She is nourished and {perfected}.

Time = 1 year {360 days}, Times = 2 OR more years, ½ Time = 6 months {1 + 2 + ½ = 3 ½ years OR 42 months, OR 1260 days}, equal time. "Is not My Way equal" (Ezek 18:25). Hence the Remnant people of God stand by the SAME 1260 days of time, times and half time, with Jesus our Offering of {30 pieces of silver} to give us our Prophetic Time of {1260 x 30 =1290}. And wasn't HE sold for {30} pieces of silver. And isn't He also our Goat for Sin, our Lamb of God who takes away sin and our atonement Ram, Who atones for our sins. But when this "time, times and half time is finished; Jesus, the Man clothed in Linen, will stand UP again and declare all "things finished" (Dan 12:6-11).

Oh yes! We are every bit a people of Prophecy today as the first two women, although their little sister is still being perfected to fulfill the days of our time, times and half time with Jesus, our High Priest in the Heavenly Sanctuary (Heb 8:1-2). Therefore, we are commanded to "look back to when the daily sacrifice was taken away"(Dan 12:11), for our 1290 days.

And so Jesus is depicted in His Death, lying between the First Two dispensations, as the women with Two Breasts Like roes (SS 4:5); simply because HE lived and died between these two dispensations; prophetically dying in the Midst (Dan 9:27). Jerusalem and the Jews before the Cross and Samaria and Gentiles after Calvary's Experience, ending with the Cleansing of the Sanctuary, "when the Gentiles time was fulfilled" (Lk 21:24-25) and the Gospel went out to a people of

the last days, as the Holy Ghost was poured

upon all flesh, for the Promise is unto

You and your children, and to all that is afar off"

(Acts 2:14-21,38-39).

So! "I charge you, O daughters of Jerusalem, that ye stir not up my Beloved, nor awake my Beloved until He pleases" (SS 8:4). But we have a little sister and she has no breast, what shall we do for her in the day when she shall be spoken for" (SS 8:8)? And that is the Answer: "In the Day when she is spoken for" which suggests that she was not yet spoken for, and that is true. Hence the infant Church of Christ today, did not stand in the days of Jews and Gentiles; which Jesus "Cut off" (Zech 13:8-9). But He has NOW made Them ONE with US in His Own BODY" (Gal 3:28-29), for "I and the Children that the Lord has given to ME are for Signs and Wonders" (Is 8:18-20).

Therefore, the Remnant of the House of Jacob, the Third Part that has been left in the land" (Zech 13:8-9) when Jesus ascended to Heaven is the infant Church of Christ, "our little sister" today;{by Signs and Wonders}, the children that His Father hath given to Him" (Is 8:17-18): and "how long to the signs and wonders"? The WORD says: "when the Man clothed in linen stands UP, for time, times and half time, all things will be finished" both sin and sinners (Dan 12:6-7]

So! She has not grown up yet, therefore

she has no breast. Thus we see Jesus on His Last

Visit to His Disciples,

before His Glorious Ascension speaking to Peter, Charging Him:

"LOVEST THOU ME" (Jn 21:14-17)

No! HE did not ask Peter Three Times, because Peter denied HIM three times, for Jesus did not and still does not play tit for tat. Salvation is serious business and Jesus did not leave the Father's Side to come all the Way to Earth to be subjected to the horrendous cruelty and shame, that he endured, just to get even; with sinners, to score a point. **HE came to save sinners.** Hence His THIRD and Last visit with His Disciples was on Purpose to discuss the Infant Church [His little lambs]that HE had just laid down His Life for because He wanted Peter to grasp the import of His Mission:

To "feed the flock of God, as an overseer"

(1 Pet 5:1-4)

So Peter! Do you love Me, **on the first Count**

"feed My Lambs" (Jn 21:14-15)

My young lambs Peter, the Infant, "our little sister". Lambs are infant sheep, who must be borne, and nurtured, even carried at times. No! she will not always do right Peter, she will not always go to the right places, or live circumspectly, walking in all the straight paths, because she is young and weak. But if you love ME Peter, You will understand how much I love Her and you will love Her too in her imperfection.

Then on the Second and Third Counts

"feed My Sheep" (Jn 21:16-17)

Sheep on the other hand, are fully grown, as the First Two Parts, Jews and Gentiles, under their Prophetic Fathers {Abraham and Isaac}, that stood under animal sacrifices. They know the Way for "their Work [by Abraham and Isaac's] was finished, and their wagons were covered" (Zech 13:8-9):

"So they brought two covered wagons

for Two of the Princes" (Num 7:3).

Hence they were Cut-Off (Zech 13:8), for they have been taught; and having already grown up, have been "sealed" (Rev 7:1-8, Eph 1:13-14) unto the Day of Redemption. So Once, Twice, "feed My sheep". But the Lambs, the "After Group, from every nation kindred, tongue and people (Rev 7:9) in the House of Jacob, that Jesus is now reigning over (Lk 1:33) comprises the THIRD Part, our little sister without breast, the Infant Church of God, that has not yet grown up. But:

> "if she be a wall, we will build upon her a palace of
>
> Silver {refined, and tried—Zech 13:9): and
>
> If she be a door, we will enclose her with boards" (SS 8:9-10).

Well! is she a Wall yet? And does she have breast now like towers? Let the WORD speak for His Beloved: For "as newborn babes in Christ desires the sincere milk of the WORD, that they may grow thereby; if so you have tasted that the LORD is gracious, to whom coming as unto a Living Stone, disallowed of men, but chosen of God and precious, you also as lively stones, are built UP a spiritual house" (1st Pet 2:2-6): and what is a house without WALLS, made up of lively stones? Lively Stones that can Praise the Lord and reflect His Righteousness to the World. Oh yes our little sister has grown up to become quite a lady, an army of believers, the Church militant, ambassadors of Heaven ; but She is still being perfected.

> So! Solomon was not just an old wise royal monarch,
>
> who doted upon his {700}wives, and {300} concubines. For he soon
>
> realized, that {700 + 300 = 1000 women}
> were all vanity and vexation
>
> of spirit. For they turned his heart away from his God.

And Oh! how the mighty have fallen, for One whom; all the earth listened to as he spoke, because of the Wisdom that God had place within his heart" (1 Kg 10: 24), became a double-crosser and a traitor of the Faith, who turned against God, to his own destruction. But, the moral of his life story serves to remind us, that to stay with God, is to have God stay with you. For, ONE greater than Solomon is now in the Garden:

Truth Amplified, Greatness Personified,

Righteousness Magnified and Redemption Solidified

as His 1000 years has been Ratified

to those who will be Glorified (Rev 20:6).

Nevertheless, it was not Solomon's 1000 women that counted to guarantee the Promise, but unto the keepers whom he hired. For 1000 pieces of silver; is as all flesh that is regarded as silver, whether they are reprobate or refined, wives or concubines. But my vineyard is Mine, the Garden of the Lord, and it is before ME:

"The LORD reigns. He sits between the Cherubim

let the earth be moved. The LORD is great in Zion, and high

above all the people, praise HIM, for His great and

terrible Name is holy" (Ps 99:1-2).

Therefore, "while Solomon had his 1000 pieces of silver", his women; those who now keep the Fruit of My Garden must also have their 200" (SS 8:12). Yes, Adam kept the Garden by his {800}, and as his children we too "must also keep the fruit of God's Garden, for our 200", if we are to honor the CROSS and wear the CROWN.

{1000 - 200 = 800}.

And what is that fruit? "I create the fruit of the lips

"Peace, peace to him that is afar off and near" (Is 57:18-21).

Therefore, when Adam ate the fruit with the lips, he lost his peace with God, and he was refused by God. So, God turned to his Seed, "for the fruit of the womb is HIS [God's]reward" (Ps 127:3). Therefore, Seth the "appointed" one, was born, when Adam was 130 yrs. Hence the importance of understanding the significance of the 130 as the Prince's offering, for Adam was a Priest and therefore as a Prince of God, he made his offering. And according to the Princes offering of {130}" (Num 7:11-13), the Six men (Ezek 9:2), by the "Six covered wagons" (Num 7:1-3), by the Six measures of barley" (Ru 3:15) stood as the foundation Keepers of the Garden and the Servers of the Sanctuary:

KEEPERS OF THE GARDEN	SERVERS OF THE SANCTUARY
ADAM and Seth {800 years between}	*Abraham, Isaac and Jacob*
Noah—Sodom & Gomorrah	*130 x 3 = 390 days of years*
the "well watered gardens"	*the first 390 days of the 490:*
(Gen 5:3, 12:10)	*(Gen 47:9, Ezek 4:3-6)*
Ending with the flood, and	*by their Pilgrimages (Ex 6: 3-8)*
Judgment to the 1st & 2nd generations.	*with JESUS.*

Hence the Pilgrimages of the THREE Covenant Holders as Princes to the Third and Fourth Generations of the Earth:

Pilgrimage 130 yrs	Pilgrimage 130yrs	Pilgrimage 130yrs
Lived: 175 yrs	Lived: 180 yrs	Lived: 147 yrs

{175+180+147=502 yrs}**

"Jacob said, the days of the years of My Pilgrimage*

are a hundred and thirty years, ... though I have not

attained to the years of my Fathers pilgrimages" (Gen 47:9)

"I AM God Almighty, who appeared unto Abraham,
Isaac and Jacob

by their Pilgrimages to establish MY Covenant with them" (Ex 6:3-7)

{502-390 = 112}**

And Seth the Keeper of the Garden lived,
912 yrs & {912 - 112** = 800}*

Jesus lived {33 yrs} and & {502 + 33 = 535} and (1335 - 535 = 800}* (Gen 5:4, Dan 12:12), hence the Race from the Beginning to the End.

And so, the Prophetic Holdings of the Triune God, which stood from Adam in the beginning, to include our little sister, our world today with Jesus, as a people of prophecy, and keepers of the Fruit of God's Garden by **800** is still relevant.

Therefore Seth and his house became keepers

of the Garden of the Lord as men began to call upon the Name of the Lord, upon the 800* years of Adam his father (Gen 5:3-4). And, we today that were afar off, are inheritors of that {800}* as we also strive to keep the fruit of peace by our {200}; honoring God the Father and Jesus the Son (the WORD). For Peace with Jesus is Peace with God the Father.

Hence the PROMISE of the 1335 days is for those who
keep the fruit (SS 8:11-14) of Peace by their 200; standing on the
foundation laid by Adam and Seth,
keepers of the Garden, from

the Beginning until Jesus comes to bring in the 1335 *days.*

Therefore, to every obedient child of God "those" who now keep the Fruit, shall be 200; representing both the Father and the Son:

ADAM {God's Son}	God {The Father}	Jesus {God the Son}
800	100	100
our Father of the Flesh	our Heavenly Father	our Spiritual Father

For it is all about God Almighty and His Two Sons

(1 Cor 15:45-48).   (800 + 200 =1000)

That we may reach the promise of "1000 years

with Jesus" (Rev 20:6). And 1000 years
is an Eternity with God:

1—One Godhead

0—Father equal Person

0—Son (WORD) equal Person

0—Holy Ghost equal Person

So "be not ignorant of THIS one thing, that a {1000} years with the LORD is as a Day when it is past" (2 Pe 3:8). For with Jesus, "a day is given for a year". And at the End of the World, HE will bring in the "blessedness of the {1335} days" (Dan 12: 7-12); as the Heavenly Sanctuary comes to an End. For the Period of Grace and Mercy will be over and the Redeemed from the THREE Parts of God's House who have lived under Abraham, Isaac and Jacob of the Third Generation and Jesus of the Fourth Generation, together will reap the Promise with their 200 [because they have honored both Jesus and the Father upon the foundation of Father Adam's 800* {200 + 800* = 1000). Hence the redeemed will live and reign with Jesus in the kingdom of Heaven.

Nevertheless, it all began with the Call of God to Father "Abraham at 75 years" (Gen 12:1-4); and it will End with The {1335} days by God's Prophetic Sign of {1260}, by the Pilgrimages of :

Abraham's - 175yrs, Isaac's - 180yrs, Jacob's - 147 yrs and Jesus 33 yrs:

{175+180+147+33= 535years}   {1335-1260=75}
{1335-**535=800**}*

Hence the "blessedness of Abraham to all

Nations (Gal 3:14-17).

For as Father of the Faith, while he lived 175yrs, it was by His Pilgrimage of 130* yrs that He received the "Blessedness for all Nations to fulfill the PROMISE

{175 - 130* = 45}**, hence the "blessedness

by {1335 - 1290 = 45}**

A "PROMISE that has not yet been; and will not be perfected" (Heb11:38-40) until Jesus comes to gather His redeemed people at the End of the World, by the {1335} days. Henceforth, as keeper of the fruit, Jesus Christ, breathed upon HIS Beloved {the Church} the Fruit of HIS Lips, His Peace, restoring the Peace of God Almighty, that was lost in Eden. Hence He says:

"My Peace I give, My Peace I leave . . ."

For HE is our Peace, who has made both One" (Eph 2:14)

So! if we are faithful to the Fruit, obeying God and honoring Jesus as Savior; then as keepers of the Garden, we too shall obtained the PROMISE of 1000 years in the Kingdom of Heaven(Rev 20:6), as we sit down in our rightful places with "Abraham, Isaac and Jacob"(Mt 8:11). Hence our Prophetic Period of Seventy Years {70} years that we are vigorously holding on to reach; and anxiously looking forward to as a promise, is not literal, but prophetic and spiritual, just as the Seventy Weeks were:

"For a thousand years in thy sight are but

Yesterday when it is past, and as a watch in the night . . . . for the days of our years are threescore and ten, and by reason of strength, they be fourscore years, yet is there sorrow . . . . So teach us to number our days . . . ." (Ps 90:4-12).

The Big mistake today though, is that we try to count

our days to reach the BIG 70,

rather than numbering our days; and there

is a BIG difference. For we cannot do the counting.

Judas was numbered, but was not counted with the Twelve (Ac 1:16-17, 13). For only the "LORD shall count, when He writes up the people" (Ps 7:6). Neither, can we reach the Seventy years, for IT is part and parcel of the thousand. Think about it, how many wicked and ungodly persons, have we not seen live beyond 70 years of this life and by the same token how many godly and upright believers are stricken, daily and we see them dying before reaching 70 years. Is God still able, is HE unjust, is HE a liar? Does He have respect to persons? Absolutely not. Then understand that Salvation and the PROMISE has absolutely nothing to do with flesh. It is a Gift given by God, through HIS Two Sons (1 Co 15:45-50):

ADAM the Earthly: Had 1000	JESUS The Lord from Glory:
years {an Eternity with God}	Repaired the Breach by
But lost it by default of 70 years	SEVENTY first by
He lived 930 yrs (Gen 5:3-5)	70 Weeks of 2300 days and
falling short by SEVENTY	and now by 70 years of 1290 days
at 130 yrs: He made His Offering	Jesus Man # 7—LAWGIVER of the
as the First Priest (Num 7:11-13)	Ten Commandments {7 x 10 = 70}*

*representing both Sanctuaries {Earthly & Heavenly}

The Offerings of the Sanctuary were 130 and 70 shekels {130+70=200} and didn't Jesus became our Sanctuary, after offering Himself as God's

Offering for Sin? Therefore, the 800 has already been served for you as a keeper of the Fruit (SS 8:12), now you must keep the 200 to meet Jesus at the Finish Line. Yes Adam made IT to {930} and Jesus came and fulfilled the {70} becoming the Sanctuary: Repairing the Breach, and Restoring the Path that we may be able to endure to the End (930 + 70 = 1000). So, who of the natural flesh can reach IT {THE PROMISE} Heb 11:38-40); but the redeemed.

And so! from Abel down to the last warrior of the Faith, "all got a *good report*". BUT the Promise? Oh no! Not until JESUS is finish serving our SEVENTY Years as High Priest in the Heavenly Sanctuary (Heb 8:1-2), to make up Adam's {930 yrs}; will HE return for OUR LITTLE SISTER: His redeemed children and they too will spend that 1000 years {THE PROMISE} with HIM (Rev 20:6) in the Kingdom of Heaven, for there will be {PEACE with God once again} and Peace in the Valley: "MAKE HASTE MY BELOVED AND BE LIKE A ROE.

FOR "THY TIME IS A TIME OF LOVE" (Ezek 16:8)

CHAPTER ELEVEN

RUNNING THE RACE TO RECEIVE THE CROWN

> "Solomon had a vineyard and let it out to keepers of the fruit for 1000 pieces of silver. MY vineyard which is MINE is before Me. Solomon must have a thousand and those that keep the fruit thereof two hundred [200]"
>
> (SS 8:11-12)

Athletes are a self-conscious, disciplined and determined class of people; who have distinguished themselves through much pain and sacrifice, rising to fame as recipients of national pride and honor, heroes in their own right. They train hard, often ignoring the desires of the flesh to lounge and enjoy the pleasures of social activities. Peculiar eaters, challenged by the pitfalls of gratifying urges of improper consumption, that weighs so heavily against them. A purpose driven lot, focused only on bringing home the goal, and the esteemed title that secures for them, the national respect of their country, the warmth of family and friends, yea even the recognition of their foes.

Many strive for the hundred meters, while others set themselves up by much hard work for the four hundred 'Dash' to master the race as gold medalist in this earthly life. Nevertheless, the glory of sportsmanship is and always will be the re-lay metes of passing on the baton from one to the other to land the gold. A race of life to every human soul; passing on the baton from one generation to another:

> "for one generation passes away, and another generation comes" (Eccl 1:4).

And such is the Race of Life, which began with Adam in Eden a long time ago. Albeit, before Adam sinned, there was no need to pass on the baton, for he and his were secured in Eden's Glorious Perfection, the Earthly Tabernacle Presence of the Godhead. They were provided for by the bounties of God's River, flowing forth from His Throne. They were commanded to "multiply and replenish the earth", to produce holy seed unto their God.

However, because of Adam's Short-Fall [SIN] all flesh have inherited the propensity to sin and have all come short of the glory of God" (Ro 3:23). And as a result of our sinful inclinations, we enjoy eating the wrong diet, which often causes us to lose out on the blessings of life, good health: "for I wish above all things that thou would prosper and be in health, even as thy soul prospers" and that was Adam's downfall. As a righteous man, "the Son of God" (Luke 3: 38), he stood elegantly tall in the glorious perfection of Omnipotence without a flaw, until that fatal day when he ate the wrong diet, and fell ["remember how thou art fallen and repent" (Rev 2:5). Albeit, Adam and Eve were the ONLY ones who could have fallen from the Glory of God; all other flesh have come short of the Glory of God {Ro 3:23}. And from that day, the essence of Time began to tick away, for the Race of Life had begun. Passing on the baton [Sin's wages which is Death], from generation to generation. For "a man that is born of a woman, has a short time to live, and the end thereof is death".

Beginning to age, since leaving the Presence of the Almighty, Adam with his wife produced their first child: "born in sin and shaped in iniquity". And following closely, their second son 'Abel' was born. These two boys grew together, each becoming proficient in their chosen careers. Cain bearing the attributes of God the Father, as a Farmer; while Abel projected Jesus Christ. For the order was to bring Me an Offering of animal's blood. But that day, as Abel offered his sacrifice, his blood was also shed. And what did God have before Him, animal's blood and human's blood. Blood and more blood, for the life is in the blood, but all flesh are not the same (1 Co 15:38), the flesh of man exceeds the flesh of beast. Hence the blood of the first human martyr for righteousness speaks. But the "Blood of Jesus speaks better than righteous Abel" (Heb 12:24). Albeit Abel's blood was shed because of Sin, but Jesus' Blood was shed for Sin. And so the dialogue, between God and Cain began, followed by the separation.

Cain, being one of the ancient men of the Sanctuary could not bear being cast out of the scope of God's Presence. After-all he had always been in the Presence of God, as his father Adam kept the temple settings before them. Yes Cain knew what was to be offered, he was trained to know, love and serve God. But in a weak moment, he dishonored his God. But Cain did not remain in his sins, no "my punishment is more than I can bear" (Gen 4:13), so he cried out and repented, and was marked by God himself for righteousness. Yes Adam sinned and was covered, and Cain sinned and was marked, just as all of God's repentant children who cry out to God for their sins are marked today: "set a mark [unto the Day of Judgment], upon the forehead of all those who sigh and cry for the abomination in the land, and begin with the ancient men of the SANCTUARY" (Ezek 9: 4-6).

And Cain was one of the Ancient men that lived before the Wilderness Sanctuary was erected. Nevertheless, "and in the process of time" (Gen 4:3), just when Eve thought all was loss, one son murdered, and the other left home, the third son was born when Adam was 130 years old. Albeit, **Adam who was created fully grown, did not age with years of time, until after he sinned and fell short of God's Glorious Perfection**. Hence he was cast out of the Glorious Habitation of the God Head. Yea! falling short of living eternally in the Presence of the Triune God. Thus Adam began the race of life; living and serving for 800 years, **after** his third Son, Seth [the appointed one] was born to set the Race for all flesh by their 200, to reach the {800 +200= 1000} at the End of Time. For a day in God's sight is as a thousand years:

THE TRIUNE GOD	ADAM AND ALL FLESH
1—One Godhead [Trinity]	Father of all flesh
0—God the Father {equal Person}	Adam served 800
0—God the Son {equal person}	each person—200 by keeping
0—God the Holy Ghost {equal Person}	the Fruit (SS 8: 12).

Thus fulfilling the Promise of (Rev 20:6), as the redeemed of Adam's race, live and reign with Christ for a [1000] years in Heaven in the Glorious Perfection of the Father. For that which was lost to man will be restored. Hence the PROMISE, a Promise that all Faith warriors are still waiting to receive (Heb 11: 38-40) from righteous Abel down to the last repentant soul (Heb 11:4-40) who keep the fruit by their 200, as Adam's redeemed children

And so, just as the first two boys of the human family grew in the grace and knowledge of knowing God and His Ways, they met their appointed test of faith at the time of the yearly sacrifice. Cain a farmer by trade thought it too ugly and messy to mingle with blood; killing young innocent Lambs year in and out. He had seen his Father Adam offered the yearly sacrifices on behalf of the family time and time again. He was tired, yea fed up with this yearly ritual. There has to be a better way. Yes a fruit! That's much easier than killing a lamb. And where would he secure a lamb from anyway. From his little brother's Flock? I don't think so, because if Abel's offering could be accepted as coming from his own hand, then as a farmer, why can't I offer the fruit of my hand. Oh the rationale we offer to God in place of obedience and surrender. But "Cain was marked, and went and dwelled in the land of the East of Eden, for "the LORD God planted a Garden East of Eden" (Gen 2:8). Yes, and there he met and married a wife, and yes he knew her, just as Adam knew his wife (Gen 4:1), yea every husband has that prerogative.

Well, where did she come from, wasn't Adam and Eve the first two created upon the Earth. And wouldn't that make Cain and Abel the third and fourth persons. So then, is the Bible a Book of make believe [lies] and fairy tales, or Truth. Albeit, "God is not a man, that He should lie" (Num 23:19), so "let God be True, and every man a liar" (Ro. 3:4). Therefore says the WORD, "whom shall I teach knowledge..."(Is 28:10-13), those who can put line upon line and precept upon precept. Hence Jesus admonished, "search the scriptures....they testify of ME" (Jn 5:39). And no! Disobedience did not breathe SEX, it breaths SIN. Sex did not begin with SIN, it was and is a Gift from God to the right people at the right time in the right place. For in the beginning, He created them male and female, and HE took the woman to the man, "and they shall be one flesh" (Gen 2:22-24). Then God commanded them to "be fruitful and multiply and replenish the earth (Gen 1:26-28), even before Sin entered their Eden Home. Yes they were man and wife, naked and was not ashamed, because their nakedness was covered under the Glorious Perfection of the Almighty. But after they sinned, "their eyes were opened and they knew that they were naked"(Gen 2:25, 3:7), and ran to seek cover under Fig leaves.

Therefore, when it is said that Adam knew his wife, the same as Cain knew his wife, it means only that they copulated together. For when one is in a right relationship with God, through Jesus Christ, he is clothed, but to sin is to become naked. Hence Jesus declares:

"ye are miserable, blind and naked" (Rev 3:17)

This was not a literal nakedness at all, but rather a call to repentance. Buy of Me, that I may clothed you. And so our first parents found themselves naked as a result of their sins; and they were punished. However, when one is punished for an act, that punishment must be something contrary to the norm; something which the guilty one knows and enjoys, must be taken away. Something that will deprive them of the sweet pleasures of the life they enjoyed. Hence the man's Punishment, was to toil and sweat in the heat of the day, rather than enjoy the cool atmosphere of Eden's Garden, working and caring for His Father's Estate. So it wasn't that he didn't work before, but the punishment made the work more intensive [because he learn to sweat] and less enjoyable (Gen 3:17-19). Likewise, where the woman bore children easily, holy seed in righteousness **to the glory of God in the East**, she must henceforth bore children in sorrow and hard labor (Gen 3:16). How would she know any other way, if she had never born children before?

So yes, Cain knew his wife, they copulated; and he became the Father, of THREE sons, {honoring the Prophetic Mold) and as one of the ancient men who dwelled [lived] before the Sanctuary (Ezek 9:6). Thus it was that Cain and his descendants projected the Sanctuary. And from the descendants of Cain who made his way back to God, in the East of Eden, figuratively the Church of God, where the Presence of God dwells, the Sanctuary stood in the East. For the Glory of God is and always will be in the East:

> "behold the glory of God came from the Way of the East" (Ezek 43:2).

> "behold that Righteous Man[Jesus] was raised up in the East" (Is 41:2).

> "And when He returns, He is coming as lighting from the East" (Mt 24:27)

> Wasn't Job also the greatest man in the [Church] "in all the East" (Job 1:3).

Hence the prophetic ram that push west, north and south, but not east, (Dan 8:4), because the East is Temple Ground. Yea! "Tidings from the East [Church] shall trouble the Beast" [Satan] (Dan 11:44). The East was God's Domain in Cain's days, and it is still so today, yea from the days of Adam.

And so the Race which began with Adam and his three sons in prophecy, continued with Noah and his three sons by prophecy. Hence the three sons of Adam and Noah fit into the prophetic mold, in the race of life:

Adam: Father of all living	Noah: Father of all Nations
Cain & Abel	Japheth & Shem (Gen 10)
Church Offering	Gentiles Jews

Thus it was, that by the descendants of Cain, shepherds, tentmakers, farmers, musicians and singers emerge through Jabal, Jubal and Tubal-Cain to service the Wilderness Tabernacle(Gen 4:19-24). For they were the "Fathers [progenitors] of such that handle cattle, and instruments, harp and organ" Gen 4:20-21] in the Sanctuary. Even as Abel, that first martyr symbolically resembled Christ, depicting the offering for sin by human blood:

> "For as the blood of Abel speak, the
>
> Blood of Christ speaks better" (Hb 12:24).

PROSE POETRY & PROPHECY   77

And by the same token, the first Two Sons of Noah, projected the First two Parts of God's House in the Earth: Jews of the East, as the people of God before the Cross, and Gentiles of the West, joint heirs together, after the Cross. So that everything prophetically and spiritually was done through the descendants of these first two Fathers. Adam the Father of all flesh and Noah, the Father of all Nations. (Gen 10: 32), of the First and Second Generations, which constituted the Church of God.

Nevertheless, "in the passage of TIME" (Gen 4:3); Mother Eve conceived again, saying I have gotten another man from the Lord" (Gen 4:1). Yes Eve felt blessed, hoping that this was the appointed one. They had deeply regretted their actions, that caused such a tragic loss, experiencing separation by death and sin first hand, at the lost of their first two Sons. And now Adam, at 130 years, a relatively young man at that time was blessed with his third son, Seth who walked in his footsteps teaching and preaching the WORD of God, with his son Enos,(Gen 4:26). For Seth's marathon began at [105] years by the birth of Enos; and together, they continued the race, working side by side for the next 800 years {105 + 800=912}, after receiving the baton from his father Adam who died at 930 years. Hence the Church in the Beginning from Adam {930 - 912 = 18}, and this is "the eighteen upon whom the Tower of Siloam fell", the Woman of eighteen years (Lk 13:1-4, 16). For though HE too was a Galilean: "suppose ye that these Galileans were sinners above all the Galileans", yet HE was a Sinless Galilean, but He was also Shiloh, "Siloam by interpretation, meaning SENT" (Jn 9:7), who's BLOOD was not only to be mingled that Season with the sacrifices; but that year, HE was the SACRIFICE, that brought the Season [Passover] to an end; as HE fell upon the Church, who sanctioned His Death. Thereby, becoming our Passover", hanging between the two thieves. And so, knowing that He was soon to be crucified as the offering for sin, He says to all repent. Yes He loosed the Woman, His Woman, the Church. For He is Shiloh (Gen 49:10), that was to come, the tower of Siloam to hide in or the Pool of Siloam to wash in.

Albeit, these Bible characters were real people with real life situations, mood swings, and acts of rebellion, just as we have in our life time. But when it was time for God to intervene, HE did so through SETH, Adam's THIRD Son and his son Enos, after him, ending with Jesus, the

Author and Finisher of the Race of Life. Moreover, by Father Adam's Short Fall, the geographical structure of the Earth changed, as a result of the removal of God's Garden Temple. Just as "the old world of Noah's day, also changed the earth's structure" (2 Pet 3:4-8), for when God visits His Earth, nothing remains the same.

And so, Father Adam had to make his offering of 130 by weight of years. Yes 'sin is Weight, hence the Call to "get rid of every weight that so easily besets us as we run with patience the race that was SET before us". Note the race is set before us, we cannot escape it, but if we look unto Jesus, the Author and Finisher of the Race, we shall endure to the End. Therefore, every child of the flesh is admonished to make it to the finish line, as a winner. And so Seth, the THIRD Son of Adam was the Prophetic One to the World, "as men began to call upon the Name of the Lord again" (Gen 4:26). Likewise, Ham the Third Son of Noah heads the heathens [sinners, and all have sinned] in the World. And that includes all flesh, unless and until they have repented and accept Jesus as Savior.

Albeit, God works through the Fruit of the womb, even to this [OUR] Generation today, for the "fruit of the womb" is God's reward (Ps 127:3). Hence the vessels of flesh that bears the WORD, His ministers that must call sinners to repentance today. Well! what else did Adam have that God needed, but his offspring the fruit of Eve's womb, [his WIFE, his own woman]. And so from Father Adam's Short Fall, the Sanctuary was projected by the offerings of the Priests {130} and of Jesus, who is the Sanctuary by {70}:

Offerings of The Sanctuary

For the Priest (s)	Jesus Himself—the Sanctuary
1 3 0 shekels (Num 7:11-13)	7 0 shekels
who represents Jesus	Man # 7, LAWGIVER of the
to the people	Ten {10} Commandments
	{7 x 10 = 70}

Henceforth, the Seventy shekels was in weight, as the offering of the Sanctuary, for Sin is weight. So the admonition is to "get rid of every weight of sin that so easily beset us running with **patience** the race that is set before us" (Heb 12: 1-2). Running not because we choose to, but because of our birth, we have entered the arena of the world's athletes, running in the race. However, it is not just running or living from day to day, we must run with **Patience,[the KEY] to make it to the finish line.** And what is this Patience? Here "is the **Patience of the saints who** keep [run with] the Commandments of God and have the FAITH of Jesus" (Rev 14:12). Now the Faith of Jesus is not as the faith of man. Jesus' Faith is based upon Obedience to His Father's Commandments. And the invincible truth is that Patience accompanies the Law, the Commandments of God.

Albeit, we cannot run with patience and carry sin in our vessel at the same time, for Sin is weight. Therefore as we run with the Commandments, the lying must drop off, the gossiping and backbiting must drop off, because we are running and shedding the weight as we go. Running with patience, the adultery, stealing and coveting must drop off, Sabbath-breaking must drop off; because we are running. Dishonor to parents and killing are all falling off. But oh Lord we need plenty of help with this one, habitually calling your Name in vain. Yes! Disobedience of each of the TEN Moral Statues must gradually cease, as we grow in grace and in the knowledge of God. Dropping, dropping, dropping as we get rid of every Sin that so easily beset us against the strides of the Race.

Albeit, the Commandments are the **BIG** ones, but the sins that so easily besets us: murder of the heart, evil thoughts, hatred, lust, covetousness, unforgiving, intemperance and such easy transgressions, that cannot be seen with the eye. Therefore we are called to get rid of every spot, and wrinkle in readiness for the Kingdom. For:

> "the fearful and unbelieving, the abominable,
>
> murderers, liars ... part" (Rev 21:8).

So! We must shed the weight, as we run with patience the race that is set before us, looking unto Jesus". For He was the Author, at the Starting line by {70}:

First by the Seventy [70] Weeks of Prophetic Years to the early Church, under the **(2300) Days** and today by the Seventy [70] Years of Prophetic Days, under **the (1290) Days**, to the Remnant Church. And He waits at the Finish Line, as the Forerunner at the End of Time, to bestow the **"Blessedness of the 1335 days" (**Dn 12:11-12). So "HOW LONG TO THE END? It shall be for time, times, and half time, when He [Satan] shall accomplish his work against the people of God [holy People], that ALL these things shall be finished" (Dan 12:6-7). And Sin [which began time] will be no more.

Yes He waits to place the CROWN of LIFE upon the heads of His redeemed Children at the Finish line. For, He was the Seventy Weeks to the early church [Jews and Gentiles] and HE is today, also the Seventy Years to the Remnant Church, urging us on, for the RACE is not to the swift, but to those who endures unto the End.

And so Father Adam, who was cut-off at **{9 3 0} years**, passed on the Baton to His successor, his Third Son Seth "as men began to call on the Name of the Lord AGAIN" (Gen 4:26). **But the race continues today with YOU and your 200.**

Running in the Race of life

Though often beset by peril and strife

Yet conquering in the fight, at will

For God's Hand is ever present still

So be strong and dauntless to the End

Your Defender waits to welcome His Friend.

CHAPTER TWELVE

THE 800 METERS

The first six athletes in the Race of Life have been appointed to run the eight hundred meters, keeping the Door of the Lord's Temple open in the First Generation of human existence upon the Earth. The number EIGHT denotes VICTORY, hence the eight hundred meters set the foundation for every soul of Adam's race to build upon, by their "two hundred {200}" Relay in the Race of Life (SS 8: 11-12), that they may be victorious to claim their Crown:

      Solomon's vineyard   VS   My Vineyard

For the Promise which comes at the End will be given by the Author and Finisher of the Faith and of all time(s), the Victor and Champion, the fore-runner, Jesus Christ, HIMSELF.

The eight hundred years marathon is clearly defined in the lives of the first Six men through the Prophetic Holding of Divinity. For it was not by chance that the years of these chosen ones; **after they produced the Lord's appointed**, were given in the accumulation of their days upon the earth. Oh no, the WORD [from Genesis to Revelation] is all inclusive and conclusive, the TRUTH by Jesus Christ. For God spoke in the beginning and it was done, hence the Plan of Salvation was laid in the Foundation pillars. So, it is not by chance that the days and years and off-springs of the founding fathers were recorded. No it is not happen stance, that the years of the lives of God's servants were recorded, for they speak of the LIFE of God's Church in the Earth. And that which God has spoken and done, is done for ever (Eccl 3:14-15)

    For "that which hath been is NOW, and

    That which is to be hath ALREADY been, and

    God requires that which is PAST"

Therefore, not one word will fail, hence the 800 years of the first Six men in the beginning:

Father Adam who began the Sin Problem made His Offering [produced Seth]

at **130** yrs and lived **800 yrs after** to 930 yrs

Seth lived 112 yrs, produced Enos and lived **800 yrs after** to 912 yrs

Enos lived 105 yrs, produced Cainan and lived **800 yrs after** to 205 yrs

Cainan lived 110 yrs, produced Mahalaleel and lived **800 yrs after** to 910 yrs

Mahalaleel lived 95 yrs, produced Jared and lived **800 yrs after** to 895 yrs

Jared lived 162 yrs, produced Enoch and lived **800 yrs after** to 961 yrs

Hence the appointed span of 800 years to the First Generation, by the Appointed of the Lord, in passing the Baton from Father to Son, and from generation to generation, is every much a part of our salvation. Therefore, every child of Adam's race has an appointment to keep by their 200 (SS 8:12) in the vineyard of the Lord which is before Him; even as the "Race has been set before us". And as keepers of the Fruit, we must pass the baton on "to our Children that they may pass it on to their Children" (Ps 78:1-10). For I am the true Vine, and my Father is the Husbandman. And every branch in me that do not bear Fruit he takes away, and every branch that bears fruit, he purges that it may bring forth more fruit" (Jn 15:1-5).

And now see the Wisdom of God, in running the Race, beginning with the appointed ones by 800 yrs. For the Church that began with the First Adam will also END with the Second Adam, God's Two Sons (1 Co 15:45-49). Therefore God has ordained that the Church from Adam's Time by 800 years after, and by his offering of 130, by Seth, will remain with the Church throughout the End of Time, climaxing "with Jesus and the Blessedness of the 1335 Days"(Dan 12:11-12).

Hence the parallel of Adam's Offering [130] the First Prince runs with God's FOUR Chief Princes to the Third and Fourth Generation "by their Pilgrimages" (Ex 6"3-8), of [130] years:

ADAM	ABRAHAM	ISSAC	JACOB	JESUS
Lived 930 yrs	Lived 175 yrs	180 yrs	147 yrs	33 yrs
Offering 130	Pilgrimage 130	130	130	40—Sacrifice
-------	----------	--------	--------	------------
800*	45**	50***	17****	1335

{1335 - 1290 = 45**} {175+180+147= 502+33 = 535}

AND

{1335 - 535 = **800***}

Abraham 45 **—Blessings upon all Nations through Faith—is the Blessedness of the {1335} Gal 3:14-15) Covenant Confirmed in Christ Dn 9:27.

Isaac 50 ***—Oath fulfilled—Pentecost—Beginning of Faith to Gentiles.

Jacob 17 ****—Jesus Christ Man # 7—LAWGIVER of Ten Commandment Law (7 + 10 = 17)—Established upon Ps 105:9-10.

Jesus and the 1335:

    1—Bridegroom coming for the Remnant of the

    3rd Part in the

    3rd Part of the House of God, representing the Church by

5 Wise Virgin depicting the Church

{1 + 3 + 3 + 5 = **12**}

In the Third Part of the House of God representing the Church at His Coming

Albeit, as a tree [YOU] must bring forth fruit spiritually, unless barren. So Jesus was ready to destroy the Fig Tree, because it bore no fruit. And prophetically, and spiritually, the Fig depicts the Peace of God and peace with God. But this Peace was destroyed by Sin, necessitating the need for a Savior, Jesus Christ who came and died to eradicate Sin. Wherefore, after restoring the PEACE of God by becoming "our Peace" (Eph 2:14), at His parting, He breathed upon His disciples [all who accepts Him], His Own (Personal) declaration of Peace:

"My Peace, I give, My Peace I leave"

It's a Personal declaration. You have destroyed my Father's Peace, now I give you My Peace, not "the Fruit of the TWO Trees in the Midst of the Garden" (Gen 3:3), but the "Fruit of the Lips" (Is 57:19), hence your 200 by honoring God the Father and the Son. For he that "keeps the Tree, honors his master" (Pro 27:19). Will you honor Jesus, your Sanctuary and His Father by your 200? Albeit as Your offering for sin he is Your [30] pieces of silver, and as Your Sanctuary, He is Your [70], your "Lawgiver, your Savior, and your coming Judge" (Is 33:22). For **all** must stand before the Judgment Seat of Christ (Ro 14:10). Henceforth, Jesus is symbolically by the {30 + 70 = 100}, the Peace of God (Eph 2:14). So, One hundred for the Father and One for the Son {100 + 100 = 200}. For to have Jesus, is to have His Father also. So will you keep My Peace, or will you destroy IT as Adam destroyed My Father's Peace? Hence the {200} meter race that each child of Adam must run in to keep Peace with God.

And to have the Son, you must also have the Father. For "I am in the Father and the Father is in Me" (Jn 14:11). "I am the true Vine and My Father is the Husbandman" And "MY vineyard is before Me. Solomon had his (1000) women of years, and I have a {1000} Years to give to My Woman My Body, My Church (Rev 20:6); and to those that keep the Fruit thereof by their two hundred [200]." (SS 8:11-12). Moreover, the first two trees in God's Garden stood together like Law and Truth, or Grace and Mercy. Albeit, when we break the laws of the Land, don't we come under the mercy and grace of the authorities of the land. Henceforth, it is written:

"he that keeps the Fig Tree, honors his Master" (Pro 27:18)

Yes!

"great Peace have they that Love thy Law, and nothing

Shall offend them" (Ps 119: 165)

Therefore, be a keeper of the Fruit, and thereby honor your Master [GOD]. For the Fruit of the Lips is Peace" (Is 57:19) with God and with man.

In every trying trail of life,

In every bitter train of strife,

Buried deep within the heart of man,

God's Peace lies dormant, to be found.

CHAPTER THIRTEEN

LOWERING THE BAR, RAISING THE STANDARD

As the "Flaming Sword" was preparing to turn into the Way of the Second Generation, the Bar was lowered, in order to raise the Standard. Going from the **appointed {800 yrs} after**, to **{700} years in time**. For the number Seven belongs to the ONE, the ONLY one, Man Number Seven, or those appointed to project Him in the Prophetic Plan of Salvation. Notwithstanding, **the Bar was lowered from {800} to {300} to raise the standard to {700}**. For a new day hath dawned, when a man, so faithful, so committed and so connected, determined he would not turn back, but continued walking with God [The Triune God]; and in faithfulness and obedience, he lived **{300} years, after** depicting the UNITY of the THREE Persons of the God Head. Walking with God, who would dare? But Enoch did and God took him. Hence the **700 meters that should have followed behind the 800** meters was intercepted by the **{300} Meter** in a one man marathon, for the "Race that is set before us". Albeit, Enoch championed the course and received the Crown, for God took him. But he left behind a sprinter, to begin the {700] Dash, Methuselah, the fruit of his loins. The longest man that ever lived, was the athlete at the commencement of the {700} Dash that led up to Completion of the Work of Salvation, by the fore-runner, Calvary's Trail Blazer, Man Number Seven in the Flesh.

Yes from 800 to 300 and back to 700, years in time, followed by another man, Lamech whose race set the stage for the Seventh Triathlon, running a race all by himself in the Seventh inning. Lamech lived 7-7-7 [777] years, bringing forth that great burning torch. For "this one shall give us comfort" (Gen 5:28-29). Henceforth, touching the Number Seven, in any shape, size or form, one must be chosen and appointed by the MAN, himself; Jesus Christ, Man Number Seven, by His Personal Identification. Notwithstanding, the number Eight was appointed and set as a Sign of Victory upon Adam's {800} and followed on to the others keepers of the Garden, until Enoch championed the Course. Oh yes, the Bar had to be lowered so that the Highest Standard of Righteousness could be set and applied, from the First Adam going down, and coming up to the Second Adam, gives the Victory of the Cross:

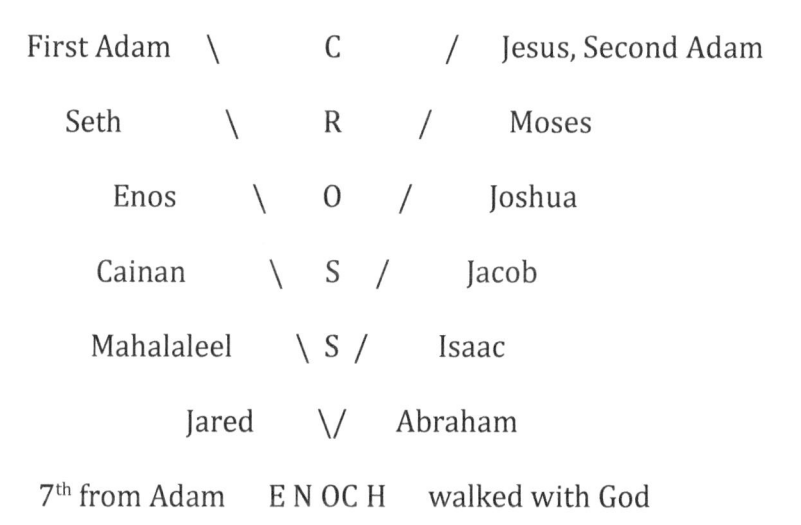

```
First Adam    \       C       /    Jesus, Second Adam

   Seth         \     R      /       Moses

    Enos         \    O     /        Joshua

     Cainan       \   S    /         Jacob

      Mahalaleel   \ S /             Isaac

        Jared       \/               Abraham

7th from Adam    E N OC H    walked with God
```

Standard bearers are one of a kind, heroes of the Faith. Their quality of life often outweighs the quantity of years. And this was the case with the Seventh Man, on the spiral down from Adam. Enoch a peculiar one, sought the company of the Godhead [Trinity], for the last 300 yrs of this life in favor of Eternal Life, there and then. Walking with God, day and night, year in and out, he became like God and could not remain on this earthly plain. So God took him, after running the Race for 300 years after, to joined with the {3} in One, Father, Son and the Holy Ghost. Passing on the Baton to his Son, the longest living man of the Earth, which began the Spiral down again from the 800th of the Victory Line; to raise the standard UP on a spiral of the 700th on the Path of the Suffering Lord, Jesus Man Number Seven, triumphing a VICTOR, to bring in the Trophy of Salvation for Adam's Children.

Another Standard Bearer, Lamech lived 595 yrs after producing the "fruit of the womb, God's reward" (Gen 5:30), ending at [777 yrs] depicting the three sevens which projected the THREE Prophetic Weeks of Twenty-One prophetic days that was to come. For "the Prince of Persia withstood ME, Twenty-One days" (Dan 10:13).

Hence the Twenty {20} days of years of Jacob and the One Day-year of Jesus to perfect the THREE Prophetic Weeks of all Prophecy, by {7 + 7 + 7}:

Jacob	Jesus
Served 2 Weeks & 6 days	Served ONE Day = 3 Weeks

Therefore, after Calvary Jesus came forth Victoriously, the triumphant Winner of the Race to "reign over Jacob's House forevermore" (Lk 1:33). Thus projecting Prophecy by the Rain that was to come "after 7 days, and He stayed 7 days by the Olive Branch in the mouth of the dove, and yet another 7 days" (Gen 7 :4, 8:10, 12); thus depicting the THREE Prophetic Weeks by: [7- 7- 7] of the Sanctuary, (Dan 9:24-24), and then HE, [the Dove of the Spirit] was gone. Bar raisers and Standard bearers were poignant in the Prophetic Holdings of Omnipotence. And oh how the people longed for ONE to bring them comfort in their sorrow and strength in their years of toiling. A Giant indeed and a Standard Bearer of Truth, a typical tyrant of righteous. A man of Faith was Noah:

"by Faith Noah, being warned of God of things to come

prepared an ARK to the saving of his house . . . ."
(Heb 11:7).

Never seen rain, or heard thunder, never experience lightening; but undauntedly, he set out to lower the Bar, and raise the Standard, by the Number Seven {7}, taking with him Seven clean animals (Gn 7: 2-3) into the Ark. Hence the Sacrifice of Praise and Thanksgiving by these SEVEN (Gen 8:20). And in a sense, Creation began all over again, keeping flesh alive upon the Earth. Yes, cast out of the Garden, but called into the ARK; was Noah's cry as he pleaded. The chiseling of the saw and the banging of the hammer bespoke the word, "Repent", echoing throughout all the land. Every drive of a nail sealed his witness to give comfort in the plight of rebellion. This "Flaming Sword" who hailed from the loins of the Man, that lived 777 years, yea Seven three times around sealed God's Promise by the Token of a Rainbow, bearing Seven {7} colors.

Blue—Remember to Obey (Num 15:38-39)

Orange—depicting Sun rays

Green—depicting herbs, grass, trees

Yellow—depicting harvest, ripening of fruits

Indigo—depicting the Purity of the heart

Purple—depicting the Majesty of Heaven and Earth

Scarlet—depicting Sin, and the Blood of Christ,

And by these Seven Colors, God Almighty staked the Salvation and Redemption of Adam's race, through the Blood of the Lamb, His Lamb, Man Number Seven; whose Blood takes away Sin. Albeit, blood leaves a stain, but this Pure and Undefiled substance from the veins of the righteous Son of God, removes all stain and leaves the foulest sinner clean. Hence the prophets view of the Throne of the Most High, with the Rainbow overshadowing it (Ezek 1:4-4-28). And today that PROMISE still brightens the Sky on a dark and cloudy day. Hence the token given to Noah and his seed, as "Father of all the Nations" (Gen 10: 32). For "as it was in the days of Noe [Noah], so will it be with the Coming of the Son of Man" (Mt 24:37-39):

Noah, Man's # is 6	Jesus, Man #7
served a life span of 120 yrs	4 months to harvest
(Gen 6: 3)	{30 x 4=120}* (Jn 4:34-35)
Harvest—8 persons	Harvest at the End of the World

4 months of 30 days = 120 Days of Years*

For it is God, who has reserved the appointed weeks of harvest (Jer 5:24), first to Noah's generation and now to Jesus' generation alike. Moreover, it was not only the token of the Bow by Seven colors, but Noah was distinguished by the Seven {7} clean animals that He offered as a sacrifice, again representing Jesus Christ, as the Ultimate Sacrifice. And finally the Man Himself, clothed in Linen with His ink horn, stands with the Six Men at the Higher Gate today; as the 7 shepherds of God in the Earth:

"and THIS Man, #7 shall be our Peace " (Mic 5:5)

"This Man" (Jn 18:29)   "Not THIS Man" (Jn 18:40)

Hence the Victory of the Cross, "THIS MAN", Jesus Christ, Man Number Seven came and brought all things to perfection and fulfillment by His Own Blood, wiping out:

The dipping of animal's blood 7 times

Wearing of the linen garment 7 days

Being sanctified for 7 days" (Lev 4:1-17)

For "this Man", shall be our Peace (Mi 5:5); having offered Himself as a ransom for Sin, thus restoring the Peace of God; by His own Lips as He breathed His Peace upon His Church: Yes! He raised the Bar, and yet lowered the score, in the Race of life; so that whosoever will may endure to the End and receive the Promise that awaits the redeemed children of God at the Finish line, a CROWN of Righteousness.

Standard Bearers, of Righteousness and Truth

Bar Raisers and Pace Setters

Pilgrim travelers on the sands of time

Garden keepers, Peace lovers, Law abiders

Rest secured within the fold of God

striving to reach that heavenly abode

CHAPTER FOUTEEN

THE FAITH RUN

Faith is a Gift of God given to every child born of Adam's race A gift of life that accompanies every faint cry on the threshold of life:

"for He has given to every man a measure of faith"

But what we do with that measure is determined by how far our faith will take us, for faith works for us or against us.

"show me your works and I will show you my faith"

But faith and works must run hand in hand, to accomplish the will of man, whether for good or for evil. Hence the Faith Run, from the cradle to the grave. For" the Race that is set before us began the count down with the fall of man; when Time began. To some were appointed the 800 year run, cheering us on to Victory in Jesus, the Messiah. A Victory of the Promise, at the End of Time, "that has NOT yet been perfected" (Heb 11:39-40). To others were appointed the Salvation Sprinters of the 700 year Dash, leading up to Christ's Sacrifice on the Cross. But today the Relay continues to the 200 meter run, as God and sinner reconcile, {One to one}, through Faith in Christ Jesus. Hence the warriors of Faith:

By faith Abel offered a more acceptable offering

By faith Enoch was translated

By faith Noah build an ARK

By faith Abraham answered the CALL

But **through** Faith, Sarah conceived. By Faith and through faith. Faith runners never move through faith, they set the standard by Faith and raise the Bar for others to move on through Faith, hence Sarah moved on through the Faith of Abraham.

By Faith Abraham offered up Isaac

By Faith Isaac blessed Jacob and Esau

By Faith Jacob blessed both the sons of Joseph,

crossing the hand to rest upon Ephraim.

By Faith Joseph command for the removal of Israel

from Egypt, including his bones.

By Faith Moses was hidden and preserved

Through Faith, they kept the Passover, **by** Faith they passed through the Red Sea, the Wall of Jericho fell, Rahab perished not, and so much more. Time would not allow to tell of Gideon, Barak, Samson, Jephtha: David, Samuel and the prophets. Who **through** Faith subdued kingdoms, wrought righteousness, obtained promises, stop the mouths of lions, quenched violence, escaped the edge of the sword, the weak made strong, men waxed valiant, chase armies, the dead raise to life: mocking, and scourging, imprisonment, all through Faith, the Faith of our Fathers, living still. They have all ran well, scoring high points in their pilgrimages, But Have Not Yet Received The Promise. A good Report, but no Promise, not YET. Because the Faith Run is still racing along, with our generation today:

> "wherefore, seeing we ALSO are compassed about with so great a cloud of witnesses, let Us lay aide every weight and the sin that doth so easily besets Us, running with patience the Race that is set before Us, looking unto Jesus, the Author and Finisher of our Faith" (Heb 12:1-2)

Running with PATIENCE, the Race? Patience for what, in what by what, will the Race be won?:

"Here is the Patience of the saints, here are

They who keep the Commandments of God

And the Faith of Jesus" (Rev 14: 12).

Running with patience, the race. Don't you see I'm running, running and dropping, dropping the weight of lies, of jealously, of stealing. Yes, I'm running and dropping adultery, disobedience to parents and Sabbath breaking. I'm running and bearing the patience of Jesus, as I keep the Commandments of God, dropping murder by the tongue, the mind and the hand. I'm putting aside the false gods, and irreverence of the Name of God, because I'm running the race that IS set before me. Trying, striving, yes struggling to make it to the Finish Line, with the Faith of Jesus, by His Creed. For I began with Jesus at the Starting Line, accepting Him as my Savior and Lord and I long to meet HIM and greet him at the Finish Line as Redeemer and King:

> So: when my ship is sailing on the
> boisterous sea of wind and strife

> When tribulation threatens, my poor soul in anguish lies

> It is then I look to Jesus, on His strong Arm I can depend, and I know that

> HE will keep me and preserve me to the end

> Jesus and Me, there's no room for three

> On His wings of Mercy, its just Jesus and Me

> In the midst of my confusion,
> when my eyes are blind with tears

> I may not feel his presence, but I know He hears and cares.

> So I call on Jesus, for I know He will see me through

He will banish disappointments, all my fears, He will subdue.

Then, as I travel on the pathways of mercy truth and light

Dark and dreary days may often be my plight

But I reach out to my Savior, He's my closest, dearest friend

And on my pilgrim voyage, it is Jesus at the Helm

In warfare He's my Contender, for He knows just how to fight

He's the Rock of my Salvation, my refuge day and night

So when my foes assail, and my strength begin to fail

He is my great Defender, in the battle He'll prevail

Jesus and Me

Running the Race and dropping the Weight,
that so easily besets me.

CHAPTER FIFTEEN

THE THREE HUNDRED METERS

One, Two, Three complete and perfect evidence, followed by Divine intervention:

> For "there are THREE that bears man's record
>
> In heaven: And there are THREE that
>
> Bears Witness in the Earth" (1 Jn 5:7-8)

On the count of THREE, God Almighty set out to reveal Himself once again to Adam's race, to the Third and Fourth generation of flesh in the earth, declaring that:

"I APPEARED UNTO ABRAHAM, UNTO ISAAC AND UNTO JACOB BY THE NAME OF GOD ALMIGHTY, BUT BY MY NAME JEHOVAH WAS I NOT KNOWN TO THEM. AND I HAVE ALSO ESTABLISHED MY COVENANT WITH THEM . . . . AND I WILL TAKE YOU TO ME FOR A PEOPLE . . ." Ex 6:3-8).

Three in Heaven and Three in the Earth unite in a horizontal and vertical Union, God and man depicting the Cross of Christ, by HIS THREE Part Legacy:

Covenant to

Abraham {the Father}

|

God the Father _____SON_____ God the Holy Ghost

Isaac   SON   The Oath

|

|

|

Jacob {Grand Son} The Law

Henceforth, the THREE In One united with the Three of One to reveal Himself, declaring:

"I AM The God of Abraham, of Isaac and

of Jacob I have establish My covenant

with them (Ex 6 :3-8)

Thus establishing the Everlasting Covenant upon the Legacy of His Three-Part House in all the Earth:

LEGACY	(Ps 105:9-10)	HOUSE
His Covenant	J	Abraham and Jews
His Oath	E	Isaac and Gentiles
His LAW	S	Jacob and Remnant
	U	

Confirmed Covenant   S   Executed Oath

Cut off in the Midst

Dan 9:27, Gal 3:17

Hence the THREE Prophetic Fathers, as servers of the Sanctuary by their Offering of {130} yeas. Can you see the parallel with Adam of his 130 years, when he made his offering at {130}? Hence the First Three hundred and ninety Days of the Seventy Weeks {130 x 3 =390} (Ez 4:4-5). For both the Prince's Offering and the Bowl of Seventy shekels {130 and 70) made up the Offering of the Sanctuary (Num 7:13):

SEVENTY WEEKS DETERMINED (Dan 9:24-27)

(and when something is determined, it is set, and fixed)

Lie upon the Left   Lie upon the Right

(Ezek 4:3-6)

Abraham - 1 3 0}   Jesus

Isaac - 130 x 3=390}   40 days (Mt 4:1-2)

Jacob - 130 - (Gen 47:9)

{390 + 40 = 430}

Therefore Seventy Weeks was fixed and set for the Earthly Sanctuary to run its course, to the First Two Parts of the House:

70 Weeks x 7 = 490 days*

And 490 - 430 = 60 Variance   -   390 + 40 + 60 = 490*

But where did the Sixty come from, but from the Offerings of the Sanctuary:

24 oxen + 60 goats, lambs, rams (Num 7:88):

Serving High Priests—made up of twelve tribes to each of the First Two Parts:

Jews	Gentiles	Jesus {The Sacrifice}
12 tribes	12 tribes	60 goats, 60 lambs, 60 rams

One goat per priest: 12 + 12 = 24 male goat [bullock] with 60 goats, lambs, rams, constituted the Offerings of the Sanctuary (Num 7:88). However, since Jesus God's Goat for Sin, God's Lamb that takes away Sin, and God's Ram that atones for Sin cannot be divided, the 60 stands as a whole to the First two Parts of the House {30 + 30}, as Joint Heirs together by the Cross, Jesus dying in the midst of them. Hence the Covenant Confirmed to Abraham, and the Oath fulfilled to Isaac, as Jesus was crucified, thus perfecting the Seventy Weeks of prophetic years to the First Two parts that was "Cut Off" (Zech 13:8-9); even as HE was "Cut-Off in the midst". Nevertheless, something else was also **determined** to take place in that One Day for a Year that Jesus Served: "the Consumption Decree for the overspreading of Desolation of the abomination" (Dan 9:27).

Wherefore since HE died in the midst of the First Two confirming the Covenant to Abraham and fulfilling the Oath to Isaac. He must also fulfill the consumption decree to the Third Part, the House of Jacob and the Remnant today. Hence He is also OUR Offering today in the Heavenly Sanctuary, by "the Value we placed upon his head" (Zech 11: 12), for HE is still Jesus, God's Offering for Sin today:

JESUS, GOD'S OFFERING by THIRTY TO HIS THREE PART HOUSE

ONE	TWO	THREE
{30	+ 30 = 60}	{30 pieces of Silver}
goats, lambs, rams: Animal's blood		Jesus' Blood
JEWS	GENTILES	REMNANT
Joint Heirs together/Cut-Off		Jesus is presently fulfilling

The Consumption Decree

That was **determined**, set and fixed by the Abomination of Desolation. For nothing takes Jesus, the Creator by surprise in His land. Thus He has warned and admonished that "when this Gospel of the Kingdom has been preached in all the nations of the world, for a witness, when therefore, ye see the abomination of desolation, spoken of by Daniel the prophet. Let him who read understand" (Mt 24:14-15). And today, we are a generation of the "overspreading of the Consumption that was DETERMNED" to the Remnant (Is 10:21-22); as the Seventy Weeks were Determined to the First Two Parts.

Hence: Jesus paid my ransom and He set me free

He bore my sins upon dark Calvary

He took my place of Sin and Disgrace and

Rescued me from Sin's Decree. Yes, He did It for Me.

When my life was ruin and my sentence given

Jesus step right in and took my plea

He offered up and drank that bitter cup

To guarantee me, a new body. Yes, He did It for Me.

Jesus suffered in agony of pain and shame

With blood flowing forth from His Hands and Feet

His broken flesh and bruised brow

Obscured the view of His darkest hour. Yes, He did It for Me

He was mocked and scourged and left to die

As that Roman spear pierced His wounded side

But He uttered not a single word

And for my sins He was crucified.

Yes, He did it for me, all alone on Calvary's tree. He did it for me, Praise God, He did it for me, that I may run the race that is set before me, successfully.

CHAPTER SIXTEEN

THE HOME STRETCH

Can you by Faith, see it in view as the path ahead blazes with the ambience of the victors, clothed in immortality. Hope chimes, as the Blessed Hope becomes a reality in anticipation of the Celebrations. Angels will gaze in awe and amazement as the blood bought triumphant throng, radiant in splendor, bearing palms of victory and wearing CROWNS of Glory, lights up in the atmospheric Glory of their Redeemer; the LAMB seated upon HIS Throne. The runners of the 800 year marathon, followed by the Bar Raiser of the Triathlon, and backed by the Standard Bearers of Salvation, all gleefully aglow with enthusiasm, that spreads an era of jubilee over the celestial horizon. No, no! the Angels cannot sing our song, hence the heavenly spectators including the twenty elders of the 144,000 of the First Two Parts (Rev 7:4-11) will gaze in amazement to behold the Remnant of the Third Part, coming in on the Home Stretch.

Yes the Vision is Glorious and the Sight is Victorious on the Home Stretch, led by our Elder Brother, the Forerunner of the Race. For HE will come to gather His trophies that are held captive today. Yes! the Lord will turn "AGAIN" the captivity of ZION (Ps 126:1-4). And note the operable word, "again", which means He has done it before. But this Time it is ZION, and where is Zion? Let The WORD speak for Himself: "where the Law of God goes forth, from the God of Jacob to a Last Day people" (Is 2:2-3, Mic 4:1-4). Yes "our mouth will be filled with laughter, and our tongue with singing, for the Lord hath done great things for us, and we are glad". Travelling on the home stretch in the 12th inning to reach the BLESSEDNESS of the {1+3+3+5=12} Days, at the Finish Line (Dan 12:12). For the sprinters of the 800 meters, the 300 triathlon, and the 700 dash, have done it all to guarantee us a safe home run. They [144,000] "have ALREADY been sealed" (Rv 7:1-8), for they were the captivity of the First Ascension; "as He ascended on high, leading captivity captive" (Eph 4:8). And they have been waiting so very long for the Day to come:

LEAH	< Jacob >	RACHEL
6 Sons		6 Sons

12 Tribal Heads constitutes the Churches' Redemption (Rev 21: 12):

First to the JEWS	Second to the Gentiles
12,000	12,000

{12 x 12 = 144,000} that have been sealed}

Hence the Walls of the City are 144,000 cubits according to the measure of a Man

And that Man is Jesus Christ, the Archangel, Michael.

Who will lead His redeemed, through the Twelve [12] Gates, named after the Twelve [12]Tribes, manned by the Twelve [12] angels, on the Twelve [12] Foundation of the [12]Twelve Apostles, to enter the City that is Twelve [12] thousand furlongs, made of all manner of precious stones, with Twelve [12] pearls, and to eat of the Tree bearing [12] manner of fruits. Yes Kingdom travelers entering their Heavenly home:

And again, for the THIRD time, God has chosen UNTO

HIMSELF a people:

"I will bring the THIRD part through the fire

And will refine them as silver and try them as gold

They shall call . . . . and I will say It is MY people . . . ."
(Zech 13:8-9)

Oh! But the Remnant, we are a people of so much weakness today, falling so far down from our fathers of 800 years, to a mere "80 or more, by reason of God's strength" (Ps 90:10), and most times, to a varying degree, even below the 70 year mark. But the battle is not for the strong, neither will the swift win the race by Years. For the RACE that has been SET before US have been conquered EQUALLY in the Battle, UPON the Legacy [THE CREED] of (Ps 105:9-10) by Dan 9:27:

(A)	C	(B)
JEWS OF	A	GENTILES of
Abraham's House	_____L_____	Isaac's House
3 ½ days	V	3 ½ days of prophetic years
Covenant Confirmed	A	Oath Fulfilled, oblations ceased
Covenant to Abraham*	R	Oath to Isaac **
	Y	

(C)

(Dan 9:27) < Consumption Decree to REMNANT >
(Is 10:21-22)

"LAW TO JACOB FOR AN EVERLASTING COVENANT"***

Hence the Remnant today are persevering,
along the pathway of life:

"Troubled but not distressed

Perplexed but not in despair

Persecuted but not forsaken

Cast down, but not destroyed" (2 Co 4:8-10)

Running the Race with the Patience of Jesus, looking to meet HIM at the Finish Line. Hear the chant for the Remnant of the Third Part, as they enter the Home Stretch. Coming out of every nation, kindred and People with our Father's Ensign;[Jacob, our Prophetic Father] in whose House we abide today (Is 2:2-30), under Jesus our Reigning Head (Lk 1: 33]. Hence the Redeemed, bearing their own national Flag Color which depicts the Coat of many colors, that Jacob gave unto Joseph, symbolic of the redeemed in the Sanctuary, from every nation; for that is God's Way (Ps 77:13-15):

"The Redeemed of Jacob and Joseph"

Therefore when Jacob gave unto Joseph, the Coat of many colors, it projected the Redemption of God's people from every Nation [National Insignia] under Heaven that will gather on the Sea of Glass. Hence the Prophecy to be fulfilled by Jesus the Stone of Israel who was destined to come through Joseph's inheritance (Gn 49:22-24) to redeemed His people. And They will be coming from the East and West, from the North and South, the Church of the Living God, wearing white robes of beauty, crowns of victory, with palms of glory. Mt ZION the Church Militant, making Her Way UP on the Home Stretch. Yes! She will conquer in the Fight, for the Battle of Righteousness over SIN and Right over Wrong, to make it with an alarming stride at the finish line. The strong will be defeated and the weak exalted at the finish line. So let us run with PATIENCE, the Race that was set before us. And "here is, the patience of the saints that keep the Commandments of God and have the FAITH of Jesus:

'Running with Jesus and sharing HIS Faith'

Sharing in the Faith of Jesus means letting go of our own faith for a faith that will not shrink, even though the foes of darkness press down upon us, trying to discourage the soul. Yes, I'm running and I' dropping the weight, getting rid of every SIN, that so easily beset me. Often discouraged and perplexed, but I'm running and dropping, bowed down with the weight and cares of life; not knowing, wondering if He hears the cry for help, or sees the tear that is shed; but I'm running and I'm dropping, the weight of Sin. Oh yes He cares, for "He who made the eye will HE not see". Yes HE sees, for His eyes are focused upon that tiny little speck of dust in His big wide universe, YOU.

So I'm running and I'm dropping the weight of being disobedience to parents, of adultery and stealing, of Sabbath breaking and desecration of God's Holy Name and of killing another, with the eye, the mouth, the heart and the hand because I'm getting rid of the weight. I'm dropping selfish pride, arrogance and temperament; such light weights that often trick the mind into believing that all is well, yet my praise cannot swell. My attitude prevents my altitude from soaring in gratitude, and thanksgiving. Nevertheless, I must run because the race is not to the swift. I may not be able to keep up with the young and strong, the academically bright, or plod along with the rich and powerful, but I have been given my 200 as a keeper of the Fruit (SS 8: 12) to take to the finish line. So I'm looking unto Jesus and I'm running. He was with me when I started out on the journey to the kingdom, and I will meet Him, the Prince of Peace at the Finish Line with the Fruit of the Lips. The Peace that guarantees that WELL DONE. My Peace I give, My Peace I leave; the Same Wonderful Peace, the Peace of God's Love.

A mind of Peace, is a mind preserved

A thought of Peace is an act of Praise

A heart of Peace is a Soul that lives

A God of Peace is a Refuge that thrills

Take that mind of Peace, and provoke a thought,

With courage bold, trusts in thy God,

And let the praises swell in joyous sounds

Of gratefulness from the heart of man.

PROLOGUE

Solomon began as a winner in the race of Life, from conception in the womb. No you will not build me a House, "Solomon thy son, he shall build my house and my courts: for I have chosen him to be my son and I will be his father" (1 Cho 28:6). A winner from the start, who matriculated in excellence with God. But he lost it all by default, as his years of life were eventually filled with merriment, lasciviousness and drunkenness. And being intoxicated by strange women, they turned his heart away from his God.

Oh yes he had his vineyard, and it was filled with women, of all sizes and descriptions. He could pick, choose and refuse at will, with 700 wives, and 300 concubines (700 + 300 = 1000), all vying for the affections of the king. Hence it is declared:

> "Solomon had a vineyard, and he let it out to keepers every one for the fruit thereof was to bring a thousand pieces of silver" (SS 8:11)

Silver, do you not know who you are, **"reprobate silver or refined silver",** which are you (Je 6:30, Ro 1:28), because one way or another you are prophetically silver (Zech 13:9, Dan 12:10). Either you are white and precious to the Husbandman [God], or depraved and a cast away by the Owner [God]. Yes Solomon had his thousand (1000) pieces of reprobate silver [strange women] and he also became a rejected instrument of God(1 Kg 11:1-11). But "ONE greater than Solomon" is now here. And He has his vineyard that he lets out to every child of Adam's race for 200 pieces of silver. Albeit, He was offered for "thirty pieces of silver" and He purchased his Woman[His Church, His Body] for "fifteen pieces of silver" {30-15 = 15} Ho 3:1-4. Hence the "fifteen pieces of silver plus 15 homers of Barley" representing His body, even as Silver represents his Flesh, [half and half] depicting the Offering{15 + 15 = 30} pieces of Silver. So, "what price would you give for me and they weighed for Him 30 pieces of Silver" (Zec 11:12), hence His Body, You, the Church.

And so, as a child of Adam's race, the victory is ours by the 800 that was set at the beginning of the race of Life, by the Father of all flesh. Nevertheless, each one must keep the Fruit of their Father's vineyard by their 200 {800 + 200= 1000} SS 8:12. Thus making you refined silver in the metaphor of Salvation, as a part of the Body of Christ, His Remnant Church today, for whom He is coming. Yes Zion, She waits militant, making her way UP on the Home Stretch.

Imagine, as She mounts Up to enter into the City, through those Twelve Gates, of the Twelve Tribes, the "possessors of the Gates"(Gen 22:17). Three on the East, Three on the West, Three on the North and Three on the South. Maybe in your earthly struggles, you possessed personal traits of unstableness like Ruben, though dignified and excelling in strength, so perhaps you will enter in through Ruben's Gate. Or maybe you struggle against cruel instincts like Simeon and Levi, and bold and quick to act like Peter. That's alright, there is none Righteous, so maybe you would enter in through Simeon and Levi's Gate to occupy your mansion on Peter's Foundation, for the Prophecy is for our Last Days. Nevertheless, we know that eye hath not seen, neither can the human mind transcend to imagine, the glories of the unknown, that awaits the Redeemed. But this we know, that thousand times ten thousand and thousand of thousands of angelic beings will witness the Grand Jubilation, of the Blood Bought Throng:

> The Vision is glorious, the Sight is victorious
> Though the Battle of Sin is still being won
> But the Promise is given to bring us to Heaven
> Through Jesus our Savior, God's Only True Son

> The Vision is coming, the End is nearing
> The 1290 Days is soon to transpire
> The Ox and the Lamb, the Bull and the Ram
> The Lion of Judah, the I AM, THAT I AM.

> The Bride is awaiting the Sound of the trumpet
> Calling the Righteous forth to arise
> Now see Him descending, the Bride Groom is coming

To receive the Blessed of the 1 3 3 5

The Church is immortalized, lose gravity to the skies
The glorified bride is now purified
Their graves are all bursting, the redeem are ascending
With shouts of Alleluias they rise.

Jesus He is Creator, Jesus He is Lawgiver,
Jesus, Our Coming Judge, our Savior, Lord
Redeemer, King of Kings

SYMBOLS OF THE POET'S SONG

The Apple Tree	The Law of God
The Fig Tree	The Peace of God
The Palm Tree	The Stature of God
The Pomegranate	The Salvation of God
The Clusters of Grapes	The Blood of Christ
The Barley	The Body of Christ
The Mandrakes	The Covenant people of God
Our Little Sister	The Infant Church of Christ
Silver	All Flesh
Reprobate Silver	Rejected of God
Refined Silver	The Tried of God
Two Breasts	Jerusalem and Samaria
Frankincense, myrrh, aloes, chief Spices	Priesthood, Death, Burial of Christ
Love Banner	The Protection of God
His Cross—His Agony	His Victory, His Creed

"FOR ONE GREATER THAN SOLOMON IS HERE"

www.ingramcontent.com/pod-product-compliance
Lightning Source LLC
LaVergne TN
LVHW090210070525
810595LV00033B/399